"The work of Brian Barcelona, One [ ]
and The Jesus Clubs is truly one th[ ]
seen firsthand the fruit of what this ministry does. *Don't Scroll* not only speaks of the way youth are accepting Christ in Generation Z through the digital platforms, but it also speaks of the heart and culture behind this movement."

—Nick Vujicic, founder, Life Without Limbs

"Coming from the 'rock 'n' roll all night and party every day' lifestyle, I'm not easily shocked, but the deception that the youth are bombarded with through corrupt societal influences is at a level I've never seen in my entire life. May this book open our eyes and break our hearts afresh for Generation Z and give us bold faith to believe for the Gospel to save millions."

—Brian "Head" Welch, co-founder, Grammy Award–winning band Korn; *New York Times* bestselling author, *Save Me from Myself*

"Brian Barcelona is calling us to join him in the gutters of social media for the sake of the Gospel and the generation that lives there. In view of Jesus' love for people who live in gutters, Brian's message deserves our attention and thoughtful consideration."

—Dalton Thomas, founder and president, Frontier Alliance International

"Brian Barcelona has reached millions with his ambition, but more than that, his integrity has allowed him to keep going. Brian desperately wants people to come to Jesus Christ and is willing to do anything to make that happen, even if it seems foolish to others, even if it's on TikTok."

—David Latting, Christian social media influencer, evangelist, and missionary

"Brian Barcelona is pioneering a new way of evangelism that is captivating the heart of Gen Z. *Don't Scroll* is a must-read for the Church. I am grateful for Brian and his team for their courage to boldly proclaim the Gospel to this next generation."

—Michael Miller, lead pastor, UPPERROOM Dallas

"After witnessing millions saved in Africa and seeing God's presence move, I can truly say that what Brian Barcelona is sharing is a move of God among young people. *Don't Scroll* is a book that I would recommend you read and live out."

—Daniel Kolenda, evangelist and president, Christ for all Nations

DON'T SCROLL

DON'T SCROLL

EVANGELISM IN
THE DIGITAL AGE

BRIAN BARCELONA

Chosen

a division of Baker Publishing Group
Minneapolis, Minnesota

Published by Chosen Books
11400 Hampshire Avenue South
Minneapolis, Minnesota 55438
www.chosenbooks.com

Chosen Books is a division of
Baker Publishing Group, Grand Rapids, Michigan

Printed in the United States of America

Library of Congress Cataloging-in-Publication Data
Names: Barcelona, Brian, author.
Title: Don't scroll : evangelism in the digital age / Brian Barcelona.
Description: Minneapolis : Chosen Books, a division of Baker Publishing Group, 2022. | Includes index.
Identifiers: LCCN 2021059246 | ISBN 9780800762445 (paperback) | ISBN 9780800762766 (casebound) | ISBN 9781493437177 (ebook)
Subjects: LCSH: Evangelistic work. | Missions. | Witness bearing (Christianity) | Smartphones. | Internet—Religious aspects—Christianity. | Church work with youth.
Classification: LCC BV3793 .B284 2022 | DDC 269/.2—dc23/eng/20220127
LC record available at https://lccn.loc.gov/2021059246

Cover design by Manny Gatian

Baker Publishing Group publications use paper produced from sustainable forestry practices and post-consumer waste whenever possible.

22 23 24 25 26 27 28   7 6 5 4 3 2 1

To my wife, Marcela,
my children
and the One Voice team.

You are the people who have been behind this book
and who have faithfully lived out these chapters.
Because of your yes since 2009, and especially in 2020,
digital missions have a road that has been paved.

Contents

Introduction

What if the next Jesus movement is digital? What if the next Explo '72—the massive youth gathering that took place in Dallas, Texas, with the late Billy Graham—is digital? What if the question posed in Isaiah 66:8 of a nation being saved in a day was God's invitation to our generation?

Crazy words from God can only be fulfilled with crazy faith that can only be carried by men and women who are crazy enough to believe that Jesus has called us for greater things.

I have heard many stories of people saying that evangelism was easy in the 1960s and 1970s. People would ask, "What time is it?" In response, Christians would say, "It's time to get saved," and people would get saved. I believe that those are the times we are in, again.

Back when my grandma was young, Christians handed out tracts, which were booklets that were about hell, sin, salvation and the Gospel message. People would flip through the pages of the tract, and it would tell the story of Jesus in a minute or less. Many people came to Christ reading those tracts.

What if I told you that the modern-day tract is not a ten-page booklet but a sixty-second video?

Every revival leader from the book of Acts onward has used the media of their time. Paul wrote letters, William J. Seymour used the printing press to advertise the Azusa Street Revival[1] and Billy Graham televised his crusades.[2] The use of media now is nothing new. A Jesus movement for which many have prayed is here.

What if I told you that the modern-day tract is not a ten-page booklet but a sixty-second video?

A fresh wave of evangelists has risen up. This time, it is not one but thousands of evangelists who are sharing the Gospel. It is not crusades built around a man people flock to hear, but it is an army of people who are dressed in ordinary clothes who have ordinary jobs living in ordinary homes who serve an extraordinary God who does extraordinary things through them.

Those ordinary people are you and me. What are we waiting for?

Jesus Is for Everyone

There was a buzz on the East Los Angeles high school campus. The week before, the Jesus Club had announced a free giveaway of the expensive Dre Beat headphones. As the lunch bell rang, we opened the doors to the gymnasium. This was the gym that a year prior God had told me He would fill with His presence.

As the doors flung open, hundreds of kids poured in. These were kids from different religions, economic backgrounds and nationalities. But they all had one thing in common: their Creator was waiting to have an encounter with them.

As we started the meeting, I did what I have done many other times. I began to preach with passion and faith. I spoke about the Gospel of Jesus Christ—the value of each person, the price Jesus paid, how Jesus defeated sin and how He now offers a new way of living.

As the time grew near for us to end the meeting, I knew that the kids were anxious for the giveaway we had promised.

After all, these Dre Beat headphones were worth hundreds of dollars. Who would not want to walk away with them? We only had one pair. So as the time was coming near to close, I stopped my message and said, "Who would like these free headphones?"

As expected, the crowd erupted with kids waving their hands in hopes that I would pick them. What they did not know was that I had taken the headphones out of the box and wrapped the empty box. After asking the crowd who wanted it, I grabbed this empty box and placed it in the middle of the gymnasium. These students got ready to jump out of their bleachers to run down.

As they expected, I said, "On the count of three, the first one to come down here and grab these headphones is going to get to walk home with them today." Before I even began to count, kids began to get out of their bleachers.

I said, "No, you need to sit down. On the count of three, the first one up here gets these." I knew in that moment the kids were going to lose their dignity. No one was going to care how they looked because there was something that they wanted.

I counted slowly, "One. Two. Three."

As soon as I said *three*, a kid who was in a gang and sitting in the front row stood up. When he stood up, everyone else sat down. With the slow walk that most gangsters have, he walked to the middle of the gym and picked up the box. I followed him with the mic in my hand and faith in my heart that God was about to do something special.

Into the microphone, I asked him to do me one favor. I asked him to open the box in front of everybody. And like a kid on Christmas, he ripped open the paper—only to find that the box was empty.

With a disappointed face, he said in front of the whole gymnasium, "This box is empty." He did not realize that he had set himself up for a great explanation of the Gospel.

I replied, "You're right. It is empty, just like your life. Without Christ you're a nicely packaged box, but you have nothing inside. Although everything may look good on the outside, you're empty on the inside."

The crowd began to make noise as though they could not believe what I had just said to this guy. I quickly said to one of my team members, "Bring me the headphones." She brought me the headphones, and I handed them to him.

He replied, "Are these real?"

I said, "Of course they're real. But I have two questions for you before you sit down."

I asked him, "Do you know me?"

He replied, "No."

"Do you deserve these headphones?" Now, that second question I asked him probably made him think a little bit more. He possibly pondered the many mistakes he had made in his life and the things he was not proud of.

He responded, "No. I don't deserve these."

I pulled the mic back to my mouth quickly and said, "That's just like the love of God. You don't know Him, you don't deserve His love, but He wants to give it to you anyway."

I handed him the headphones, and he took his seat. I knew at this moment that God was about to do something special. His presence filled that gym. And through this simple example, people understood that the gift of God—salvation—was available for them. They understood that knowing God prior or deserving His love were not qualifications for receiving salvation.

With boldness I yelled into the mic, "If you walked into this room and you've never received Christ, there is a free gift of salvation today. You may have walked in here broken, but you can leave healed. You may have walked in here depressed, but you can be set free." As I looked at the crowd, I could see hope in their eyes.

I said, "If you've never received Christ and you would like to, on the count of three I want you to stand. Do not bow your heads or close your eyes on the greatest decision you're going to make."

And as I did before when I counted for them to run up and get the headphones, I counted to three for them to come and receive a gift that would not break, that would not rust and that would not become outdated or old. This was a gift that was given, a gift that was slain before the foundations of the earth. This was the gift of Jesus. As I began to count, my heart began to pound. Would they respond?

"One. Two. Three."

As I said *three*, the response of the room was not what I expected. Nobody stood up. But it was not because they were not compelled or eager to receive this gift of Jesus. It was as if they were waiting to see who would go first. It seemed as if only after that first person would stand that they would have permission.

The long silence was finally broken by the gang member who had received the headphones. As he stood up and began to make his way toward me, he was joined quickly by more than four hundred others. I remember the sound of hundreds of shoes thundering the bleachers as kids came down. They circled me, and together we prayed the prayer of faith—an invitation for Jesus to be Lord and Savior in their lives and for them to follow Him wholeheartedly.

That day many were added to the Body of Christ. Jesus became available for anyone who was willing to follow Him. Why? Because the Gospel is for everyone.

From Darkness to Light

Have you ever wondered what it looks like in the spiritual realm when a soul comes out of the kingdom of darkness into the Kingdom of light?

On earth, we see it in the form of someone choosing to follow Jesus through an altar call or a personal prayer proclaiming Jesus as Savior and Lord. But since God created both the visible and the invisible, that transaction must be one of the greatest spiritual battle scenes in world history. When the disciples went out, preached and then came back to Jesus excited about what they had seen, Jesus said, "I watched Satan fall from heaven like lightning" (Luke 10:18). Jesus responded to their natural actions of preaching and casting out demons with something that took place in the spirit realm. He pointed out that Satan's domain fell as the Gospel went forth.

Every time someone chooses to follow Jesus, his or her choice extends much further than words that are whispered in a prayer. As weak as our yes is, it is still a yes to God. This yes breaks the hold of the ancient demonic realm that has been here from the beginning of time. In a moment, we become seated with Christ in high places (see Ephesians 2:6).

In a moment, we are grafted into the family of God. In a moment, we become kings and priests. We who were once sinners and enemies of God are now His friends. The heavenly Father rescues us from the domain of darkness and transfers us into the Kingdom of His beloved Son (see Colossians 1:13).

I love that the Bible paints for us this picture of salvation as an epic rescue moment from the kingdom and domain of darkness. In the natural, however, it could be as simple and as powerful as a few stories that I will share with you.

The message I want you to get is that Jesus is for everyone, and He comes to people in many ways. Whether you or a person you love comes from a background of atheism or another religion, there is hope. Jesus loves you and welcomes you to come to Him.

I have seen Jesus meet people in public high schools, in church services, at skate parks, in restaurants, and, in the past two years, on TikTok and Instagram. He meets people where they are and however they need to experience Him.

Whether you or a person you love comes from a background of atheism or another religion, there is hope. Jesus loves you and welcomes you to come to Him.

God's methods change consistently. He is not boxed into a system or a particular method. If we understand this, we will understand why He is now moving using digital platforms. The stories you will read in this book are all unique. They are from people who come from totally different lives, backgrounds and cultures. What is the common theme? Jesus is for everyone! Even a child can encounter almighty God.

Let the Little Children Come

When, Zoe, my oldest, was three, she hopped into the car excited about something that had happened earlier in the day. "Dad, you will not believe what happened today. I had so much fear. When I told Mommy, she said Jesus would take away my fear if I would give my life to Him." This is true, of course, since perfect love casts out fear (see 1 John 4:18). I said, "Go on. What happened?" With great joy, Zoe began to tell me how she had asked Jesus into her heart and that she wanted to follow Him. She talked about this decision so simply, not really realizing what had happened. She did not understand that she had been ripped from the kingdom of hell and welcomed into the Kingdom of light.

As she told me this, my heart nearly burst with joy.

I said, "That's amazing! You'll never regret giving your life to Jesus. I'm so proud of you. Jesus will never leave you nor forsake you."

For those of you who would ask, "How can a child know of the decision they are making?" remember that salvation has little to do with your mind and much to do with your heart. There is a reason you believe in your heart and confess with your mouth that Jesus is Lord. But nowhere does that verse say that your mind plays a part in your salvation. Jesus welcomes the young and innocent who come to Him in simplicity and faith.

As I spoke with Zoe, I could not help recalling when I was her age. Memories flooded my mind as I tried to recall one godly moment from my childhood, but I could not think of any. I only remembered experiencing depression and sadness. I could only think of the times I had sat in a corner screaming, angry at all the things I had grown up seeing. I remembered the times when I wanted to end my life, because I thought everything was my fault. I recalled the period around age fifteen when I spent time in a hospital because I stopped eating and developed anorexia. My life had been very different from Zoe's. I did not grow up with an ideal home situation.

Godless and Broken

Before I share my story, I want to say that my father and mother were young and did their best. Today they are both amazing, changed and loving parents who have grown so much, and I honor them. Most of what I went through as a child was because our home was godless and broken.

I was a surprise to everyone but God. My mom was fifteen, and my dad was a few years older. When they found out my mom was pregnant, from what I have been told, they were both terrified to tell their parents, because they did not know how they would react. That fear was so strong that they ran away from San Jose, California, to Anaheim, California, nearly six hours away by car.

My mom told me that they loaded up my dad's blue Ford truck with his camper shell on the back and just drove. They did not tell anyone they were leaving. When they arrived, my parents had no money and no place but the camper shell to live. Being the hard worker that he is, my dad got a job at a grocery store working night shifts while my mom slept in the car.

What I remember the most from my childhood is my parents fighting, the anger, the yelling and the times when I felt worthless. I did not have a godly father or mother at that time. I do not ever remember feeling safe. And I thought my parents' situation was my fault. After all, if I had not been born, they would not have been in all this trouble.

My younger brother came into the world, but that was still not enough to get my parents to love each other. After all, they were missing the One who is love.

Although my family was majorly dysfunctional and full of brokenness, it still was my family. I dreamed of my dad and mom getting along and loving my brother and me. Somewhere deep inside the kid who would cry himself to sleep was a small flame of hope that having a normal family was possible.

But things only got worse. When I was nine, after many years of seeing my parents not getting along, they decided to get a divorce.

Divorce, no matter the reason, destroys. Among its many casualties are the children. I am not saying that you should remain in a bad home situation if you are in one, but the moment a divorce happens, everything within a child that dreamed of change, every ounce of hope that they would have a normal life, and every bit of faith for a loving home is gone.

To think that divorce does not affect children too much could not be further from the truth. It does not simply affect children; it destroys them. And although these words seem very strong, this was the reality of my life before Christ. It is important that you understand that truth as you read this, because this has been what has kept me in the faith all these years. I am thankful for where Jesus has brought me, but I am more grateful for what He has taken me out of.

The word *divorce* ripped all hope from my life. What seemed like years of court battles quickly shifted everything I knew. Finally, my dad won the court case, and the every-other-weekend cycle began. If you do not know what that term means, that is when a child's parents become divorced. and the child sees one of his or her parents every other weekend.

Through a series of unfortunate events and lies, I found myself no longer believing that my mom loved me. I did not see or hear from her for five years. That was from the ages of ten to fifteen.

Fast-forward—I am fifteen and am hanging out with the wrong crowd. While at an event with my friends, I ran into someone I did not expect to see. It was Lupe, my old babysitter.

"Your mom has been looking for you!" Lupe told me. "She's been sending cards and calling." As she said that, I could not recall one call or card in those five years.

"Lupe," I said, "let me call my mom." And although I was nervous because we had not spoken in so long, I felt a wave of emotions. Anger, confusion, but deep down inside I wanted to know if this was true. Did my mom really want to talk to me and see me? Because what I had heard was the complete opposite.

As the phone rang, it was as if the world around me slowed down. I was about to hear the voice of my mom for the first time in five years, and she was about to hear mine. The ringing stopped with the answering of the phone from my stepdad saying hello. With very few words exchanged between us, I told him it was Brian. He called my mom over and passed the phone to her. We both immediately started weeping.

"I have to see you," I said. We set up a time to secretly meet in a park near my home so nobody would find out. I borrowed phones from my friends at school that whole next week so that I could call my mom.

And that week, my mom and I talked about a way that I could spend the next weekend with her. We came up with a plan. She was going to come to my house on the weekend when she had visitation rights to pick me up. Many dramatic things happened the Saturday that she showed up, things that would change my life over the next two years. But pressing through great fear and anxiety, I walked out of the home I had lived at with my dad and away from years of hurt and pain.

That day was so much like the day I got saved. In my salvation experience, Jesus brought me out of the life I had once lived and to the place of freedom.

Over the years and through many tears, my father and I reconciled. I honor him and am very thankful that God chose him to be my dad. But little did I know that move would lead me to the most epic encounter I would have with God about a year later.

My life and my daughter's life both point to the goodness of God. We demonstrate that Jesus truly is for everyone, regardless of what kind of background you come from.

Jesus Seeks and Saves

After preaching many years in schools and seeing Jesus encounter kids in gyms, auditoriums, cafeterias and hallways, I felt as if I had seen it all. I believed that I had, until 2019, when a phone call with my sister would show me that Jesus does not move the same way in each person's life.

One night, as I sat on the couch with my wife watching a movie, my wife randomly said, "When is the last time you talked to your sister?"

"It's been a while," I said.

"Why don't we invite her over?"

"I don't think she'd want to come."

"Why don't we try?"

I said, "If you want to invite her, feel free," hoping that the conversation would end there. I felt as if I had failed my sister as an older brother. I had spent many years traveling and preaching, but I did not know how to love my family well.

My wife, however, asked for my phone and called my sister. I was sure she would not answer. After all, it had been a while since we had talked. Nothing bad had happened, but life had gotten busy. To my great surprise, she picked up.

I could hear them talking, catching up and laughing. Even still, I believed that my sister surely would not come all the way to Los Angeles to see me. After my wife invited my sister, I was shocked when she said she would love to come visit us. Still not believing this, I thought that she would come for only a day.

My thoughts were interrupted by my wife as she said, "Why don't you come for four days?"

Four? I thought. *That is such a long time. What will I talk to my sister about for four days?* We agreed that in about a week she would fly to my home in Los Angeles.

I did not know why God was reconnecting us or what He was going to do, but as the day of her visit drew near, I recognized a sense in my heart that He was going to do something special.

When we picked my sister up, my first impression was that she was no longer the little girl I'd grown up with. She was now eighteen. From what she shared with me, she had dabbled in alcohol and drugs and had been in a relationship with a woman for the past two years. After hearing what my sister had gone through and the pain she had endured, I could see why she had made some of the choices that she did. At that moment, though, I did not see any of that. I just saw my sister—hurt, broken and fatherless. My heart moved deeply with compassion. I wondered, *What I have been doing all these years? I have been preaching to so many people, yet my own sister is lost.*

We began with small talk as we drove through the dense Los Angeles traffic. When we arrived at my home in Pasadena, California, I unloaded her bags. We spent the day together having random conversations, laughing and reliving memories. But in the back of my mind, I wondered, *How did my sister arrive at this place?* I wondered how the enemy had worked so hard to destroy her life. He must have anticipated the greatness my sister would live out.

That night, we sat on the couch and talked for hours. My sister poured out her heart about things she had gone through and the trauma she had experienced. I was so moved that my response was to run into my bedroom, wake up my wife and ask, "Honey, can my sister stay a few more days than planned? I really believe God wants to meet her."

Being the incredible woman she is, my wife said, "Of course."

That four-day trip turned into four weeks. And within those four weeks, I would see that God does not act with cookie-cutter responses to our individual troubles. I would witness one of the greatest miracles I had seen. At the time, I did not realize that this story would give me language to describe what I would live out in 2020.

God met my sister in the most unlikely place. One night, I felt prompted by the Holy Spirit to talk with her about the Gospel. Terrified to go by myself, I grabbed my wife. I walked to my sister's bedroom and knocked on the door.

With a loud voice she yelled, "What do you want?"

"It's Brian. Can we talk?"

I could hear her through the door getting off a phone call with her girlfriend, saying, "It's my brother, let me call you back."

My wife and I walked into the room and sat on the floor. I began to share what Jesus had done in my life. There was no altar, no worship team, no lights and no piano player like most services we attend. It was just my sister, my wife, me and Jesus. After sharing the Gospel with my sister, I asked her what I had asked many people over many years.

"Zelia, would you like to accept Christ? Would you be open to giving Him your life and following Him?"

With tears in her eyes, she put her head down and said, "Why would God want me? Look at me. I drink, and I'm in a lesbian relationship. Why would God want this?" I began to cry as I felt God share His heart with me in that moment.

I said, "Jesus made the decision that He wanted you two thousand years ago."

And on the floor of that bedroom, my sister received Christ. Not long after that, she went to Kona, Hawaii, to complete a Discipleship Training School at Youth With a Mission (YWAM). It was there that she ended the relationship with her girlfriend and began to follow Christ. I could not be prouder of her. I know that she is still on the journey of God mending her heart and discovering who she is in Christ, but I hope she knows that she is one of the greatest threats to the kingdom of hell, and that her life is one of the greatest signs and wonders I have ever witnessed.

There are moments when God does things differently. There are times when He chooses to break all the rules that we think He needs to follow. The story of my sister has marked me forever, because God did not meet her in the place I thought He would. He did not meet her at a conference or in a church. He met her in a home with a family.

Jesus Draws Close to the Lost

When God desires to draw close to those who are lost, He will meet them where they are. To the disciples, for example, who understood the world of fishing, He told them they would be fishers of men. He related His message to something they understood.

Jesus did this many times in parables. In one example, He related His vast, mighty and humanly incomprehensible Kingdom to something as simple as a mustard seed (see Matthew 13:31–32). If Jesus walked the earth today and wanted His message to be understood by everyone, He might speak about a video or an app as opposed to a mustard seed.

When God desires to draw close to those who are lost, He will meet them where they are.

Jesus always put Himself in dark places without compromising His light. You can see this by observing in Scripture the people He chose to hang out with, whether it was prostitutes or tax collectors. He brought light into every situation He was in.

Jesus was always about diversity and getting His message to everyone. You could see that by the image of the cross. The inscription above Jesus' head was translated into three different languages (see John 19:20). To me, that screams that He wants as many people to know about Him as possible.

What would you say if I told you that Jesus would not reach this present generation by riding in on a donkey, but He would get their attention by riding in through social media? What if His hands and feet stretched into the digital space?

We are living in a digital generation, so if Jesus truly is for everyone, then maybe the digital space is part of Jesus' Great Commission in which He said to go (see Matthew 28:18–20). He instructed us to go to Jerusalem, Judea, Samaria and the ends of the earth. What if the way to get the Gospel out to the ends of the earth is not limited to horseback or even a plane? What if it is through your phone?

YOUR DIGITAL MISSION

You cannot win people to Christ if you are angry with them or offended by them. Nor can you truly understand God's love for someone until you have received God's heart for them. Stop for a moment and pray this with me:

Jesus, I ask that You give me Your eyes to see and Your ears to hear. Forgive me for any offense I have carried against my family or my friends who do not know You. Forgive me for not giving mercy when I should have.

Forgive me for being angry at people for not looking like or acting like Jesus, whom they have never met. Give me Your compassion that You demonstrated in Matthew 9, and let me be the laborer who is sent. In Jesus' name, Amen.

Write down the names of three people you are believing God to save. I believe that as you read this book, He is going to give you the method they need to see the Gospel have an impact on their lives. Commit to pray for these people, and look for ways to share the Gospel with them before you finish reading this book.

Go to brianbarcelona.com/dontscroll/ if you would like to hear my testimony live. I hope it encourages you to be bold and to share your testimony with others, as well.

Live with No Plan B

Discouragement can be the greatest cancer to the faith of a believer. It always seems to come at the worst time. It is often the last blow to a believer who has already been hit by many other things. Discouragement is inevitable. In fact, there is no way to avoid it. But the way we overcome it is to never let what comes at us dwell within us.

For all the great stories that I could share, for all the moments of faith that I have had, for all the times I have seen Jesus save a soul, heal a sick body and move in ways I had previously only read about, I would have double the stories of discouragement to share. Faith and discouragement often run parallel with each other.

If you can keep discouragement from getting the best of you, you can and will fulfill the call of God on your life. Your faith should be active and not passive. Satan is not afraid of someone who believes *in* God. He is afraid of those who believe God.

If Satan can stop you with mere discouragement, it is as if he has pulled the seed of truth out of the soil before it ever had a chance to bear fruit. No matter what you are facing right now, I believe that this message has come to you at the right time.

Do not quit.

Do not walk away from where God has placed you.

Your faith should be active and not passive.

There is a reason this book fell into your hands.

Living with no Plan B is the only lifestyle of a Christian. There are two ways you live as a believer. You can live safely, or you can live sent. But you cannot do both.

Please think for a moment about the prison cells that the apostles sat in (see Acts 16:23–24). They were dark, cold and lonely. The apostles had chains binding them that stripped them of their freedom. I can only imagine the questions they must have pondered. *If I serve God, then why do I suffer so much?*

If discouragement remains in the life of a believer too long, if it is not shoved out with faith, then it is no longer outward prisons that hold him or her down. What holds believers down is the internal prison that discouragement creates.

The ability that the apostles had to sing in spite of their chains makes sense now. Their prison doors were flung open because of their faith (see verses 25–26). When faith presses past discouragement, a fragrance rises to the One who sits on the throne.

Other than mentioning a great earthquake, the Bible gives no explanation as to what opened the prison gates. I would like to imagine that it was the faith of those apostles that caused the hand of God to come down and shake the foundations that He had spoken into existence thousands of years before. I imagine that as praise and faith replaced discouragement and hopelessness, Jesus walked into that prison cell.

Remember that Jesus loves to break people out of prisons. The gates, although tightly shut, began to rattle at the sound of their song. The other inmates listened and were likely confused at the joy that was displayed by the apostles. Suddenly, the doors were flung open. But instead of eagerly escaping, the apostles sat contentedly (see verse 28). They were already free. Their chains of discouragement had been broken long ago. They considered it all joy to face trials of many kinds (see James 1:2).

If you plan to make it to the end of your life while remaining in faith, you must begin to embrace this. You must begin to understand that trials and tribulations cannot be prayed away, because Jesus promised that we would undergo them (see John 16:33). If you walk under the wings of the Most High, you will come to a point where discouragement can no longer overwhelm you.

When faith presses past discouragement, a fragrance rises to the One who sits on the throne.

You may be wondering what this has to do with digital missions and evangelism. If you are knocked out by discouragement, you will never have the opportunity to evangelize or preach digitally. And if you live a compartmentalized life in which you are trying to please everyone, you will fall into the trap of hypocrisy.

The times in which we are living demand a different breed of Christians—ones who wholeheartedly love God and who look at the cost set before them and consider it a joy.

I have watched some of my closest friends, people who had mighty calls of God on their lives, who preached, led worship and were involved in ministry and missions, slowly lose the faith and the calling they once had. The devil is strategic. He does not do things overnight. Instead, he takes his time chipping away at our faith with one disappointment after another, hoping to gain his prize at the end of our lives: an eternity with him.

Discouragement and doubt are not accidental situations you go through. They are intentional, direct assaults on the faith that you carry in Jesus Christ. More than teaching you about how to remain in the assignment that God has given you, I want to encourage you how to remain in the faith. Because if I teach you to remain in your assignment, that does not guarantee you will remain in your faith. But if I teach you to remain in your faith, it is guaranteed you will remain in your assignment.

One of the most encouraging verses I have clung to for many years is, "For though the righteous fall seven times, they rise again, but the wicked stumble when calamity strikes" (Proverbs 24:16 NIV). I love this verse because it paints the picture that even the righteous mess up. Even Christians fail. We do not always live up to the Bible stories we hear on Sunday mornings. In fact, those stories sometimes discourage us, because we feel as if those lives in the Bible are unobtainable. But the truth is that the stories of the heroes in the faith are filled with human failure.

Consider Moses, who was left by his mother to be raised by a wicked government under Pharaoh. He was a Hebrew who lived in the house of an Egyptian. After murdering a man, he fled Egypt and became a Midianite. Talk about an identity crisis. Yet he wrote several vital books of the Old Testament and delivered the Ten Commandments to the Israelites after spending time directly in the presence of God.

Let's also look at David, who had a great victory early in his life. This victory gained him the kingdom and the king's daughter. After seeing God continually show up, after prophets gave him words of wisdom and after he had every worldly thing he could imagine, he still committed adultery and murder. It is one thing to fail before God does something in your life, but it is another thing to fail when He has provided for you.

Even in his story, however, it is clear that David was a man after God's own heart (see Acts 13:22). What do the apostles, Moses and David have in common? They did not quit. Although discouragement lay at their door many times, they never let it in fully. And their lives, their successes and their failures now give faith to us as a Church that we, too, can make it if we do not quit.

Do you see how vital your yes is? Do you see how vital living with no Plan B is? Living with no Plan B activates a type of faith that can only be obtained when you live a risk-taking life.

Maybe you want to quit. Maybe you feel burned out. Maybe you are reading this book because it is your last hope that God still has a plan for your life. If you have failed, welcome to the club. If all the failures of the men and women of God were recorded in the Bible, it would probably take us a lifetime to read.

Be encouraged, because your journey is not over. You will not be remembered for how you started. In Jesus' name, you will be remembered for how you finished.

Looking back, I can see that the discouragement I went through in my younger years was a direct assault on what was coming in my life with digital missions. Before I went from reaching thousands to millions, there was a standoff between my life and the enemy. Satan may not be afraid of who we are, but he is afraid of what we are about to birth.

Christianity Is Not Comfortable

Since 2009, I have preached the Gospel to youth on campuses all over America.[1] I spent my twenties preaching about Jesus at camps, conferences and conventions. I have preached underneath liquor stores, in churches, in stadiums and in many other places. At eighteen, I was a boy with no ministry background, with no Christian father and—in my early days in the faith—no Christian mother. Most of what I learned was from the men and women in my life whom God had given to teach me.

I had become a Christian at the age of sixteen, but I struggled most of my early years in my walk with God. I did not struggle with believing in Him, and I did not struggle with knowing that He was real. My struggle was believing that He could be real in my life. I did not doubt He could heal others, and I never questioned He could save others. But could the grace of God really be real for me?

This is one of the greatest weapons the enemy uses against believers. To believe a Gospel that only has the power to work in someone else's life but not your own is not to believe the Gospel at all. This lie allows you to sit in church every Sunday, maybe lift a hand or two, say amen to the message but never truly believe that God wants to do something for you.

I believe that lie is going to stop today as you read this. If letters from apostles could change cities, if the encouragement of Paul could break division and bad theology of churches, then I believe Jesus can speak to you now through the simple words on these pages.

After ten years of preaching to young people, I found myself at a place I never thought I would be. By 2019 I had traveled the world, written a book and seen God move in ways I had only dreamed of. I was married, had two children and was part of an incredible ministry. But something was missing.

I felt overwhelmed by the day-to-day routine. I felt, in a way, bored in my faith. I would ask God from time to time if there was anything else. The ministry world did not satisfy my soul. The number of people I preached to did not satisfy. Any money I made did not satisfy. I felt the burden of working with people begin to grow.

Both your mess and your success can bring discouragement. Regardless of where it comes from, discouragement is there to take you out from where God has placed you and put you in a place that is not His will. Even scarier, discouragement is there to cause you to settle for less than the fullness of God's purpose for your life.

After a decade of being faithful to the call of God, I did not know if I wanted to continue. There was nothing in my life that was deterring me except pure discouragement. No, I did not want to leave the Lord. No, I did not want to leave the Church. I was at a place where I no longer wanted to pursue my calling, which was reaching youth. I no longer wanted to give my life to see young people saved.

There would be many nights when I would lie in my bed asking myself, *Is this worth it? Is it worth it spending so much time with other people?* I felt as if I was failing as a father and a husband because all my time was given to so many other places. *Was this really worth it?*

It was October of 2019 that I felt the worst. Ironically, I was in Disneyland, the happiest place on earth, eating cheese-filled pretzels. I thought to myself, *This is the life. Maybe I should stop preaching and work here. I could pay my bills, have my family and not have to worry about anybody else.*

See what a subtle attack that was?

I was not running to sin; I was running to comfort. I wanted a Christianity that had no cost. I wanted to follow Jesus without having to pay the price. It simply does not work that way.

Those whom God uses the most sometimes seem to be wounded the most. Ever wonder why? Many people only see the strengths of leaders and pastors. They see them preach powerful messages, and they see them in highlights on social media. But remember this: all great moments come at the price of great weakness.

The greater the power of God that flows through you simply means your weakness is that much greater. His power is perfected in our weakness (see 2 Corinthians 12:9).

Although discouragement is a tool in the hands of the devil, the devil always overplays his hand. We must remember that God not only can redeem what was meant to hurt us, but He will also use it to make us stronger.

As 2019 closed, I never would have imagined what would come in 2020. I remember finishing out that year thinking to myself, *The worst is behind me. A new season is coming.* And oh, did a new season come.

The Battle before Breakthrough

All the great heroes of the faith carry one thing in common: before the greatest moment in their lives, there was great turmoil and discouragement. Moses felt discouraged when God sent him back to the land of slavery (see Exodus 3:10–11). Esther had to anticipate risking her life by going before a king (see Esther 5:1–4). Mary endured public shame and humiliation for bearing a child out of wedlock (see Matthew 1:18–19). You cannot always see breakthrough beyond the hardships of discouragement.

Many of us use seasons of discouragement as our excuse to quit working in the place, in the calling and with the people where God placed us. I mean, who would blame us, right? Life is hard, relationships are rocky and money is short. What a perfect excuse to leave where God placed you. No one would say anything. You would have every right.

This has been the death of many callings. We have had too many "rights" as believers. We have quit when we should have pressed in. We have slandered when we should have honored. We have taken when we should have given. We have complained when we should have given thanks. We have doubted when we should have trusted. To top it off, we have blamed God. We have believed that the outcome of that season was His fault, instead of realizing that the seeds we plant will bear fruit in due time. I pray that you feel encouraged to know that these kinds of struggles are extremely normal, and they always come before the biggest moments of success.

After a rough year, I was hopeful that 2020 would be the best year of my life. After all, that is what every sermon was about in December 2019. Every pastor and preacher in church and on social media said 2020 would be the greatest year of our lives. The year of stadiums and gatherings.

As we prepared to move into our new house in March of 2020, I was ecstatic to transition into this new season. It was not long after that I picked up the keys, and we walked into our new house. It was not big, but it was ours. I had dreams to see my family grow here. We had our own space for the first time in many years, and our son was on the way.

We were in the house for maybe four days when the California governor announced that all public gatherings would be shut down. No gatherings over 250, we were told. That number quickly dwindled to fifty and then to zero.

I knew it was just a matter of time before he would announce the closing of schools. The second-largest school district in the country, the Los Angeles Unified School District, soon shut down. For most people, this would not mean much other than their kids not going to school. For me, this had significant meaning, because I had spent the last twelve years of my life preaching in public schools.

Thousands of thoughts flooded my mind. What would we do now for ministry? How would we reach people? What does a campus mission movement like One Voice do when everything is shut down? I am not going to lie—I thought, *Well, maybe it is time. Maybe this is the Lord releasing me.*

Often, hard moments are meant to grow us. Unfortunately, we have grown accustomed to getting out of them by saying things such as, "The Lord has released me," or "I am transitioning," or—even worse—"I do not have grace for this anymore." Last I checked, I have not seen those words used by the apostles or by Jesus.

We have created a culture that runs from the hardships that are meant to purify our faith. And there I was, falling into those phrases and hoping I would somehow be released from what He had called me to do. God had told me He would save every school, but maybe He had changed His mind.

> **We have created a culture that runs from the hardships that are meant to purify our faith.**

The following few months were the hardest as Los Angeles County locked down completely. All my traveling was canceled. And for the first time in a decade, I was stuck. At home. With no option but to face myself.

I could not escape to travel and preach; instead, I had to take a hard look at who I was without any of the ministry that I did. That season was not filled with prayer, fasting or much Bible reading. I filled it with complaints, anger, frustration, discouragement, shame and the feeling that I had failed as a leader. I truly had to face the fact that I had no Plan B. I indulged the next months on food, video games and pure boredom.

Maybe 2020 was not like that for you, but it was for me. Little did I know that these circumstances would soon become the fertile soil for my faith to grow again.

God Still Sticks with Plan A

I had lived the last decade with no Plan B. I had given one hundred percent of myself to what God had asked. Yet here I was feeling confused. Did God not know? Did He not understand that every school had shut down? Why would He call me to do something that would fail? Why would He want to make me look stupid?

God uses humble and broken men and women. He was setting the stage to truly write history with my life. I wrestled from March to June. What kept me together was my wife, who was praying, reading, encouraging and at times rebuking. Her voice was the only way that I heard God that year. She could have never guessed how her small encouragements, prayers and faith would be catalytic to launching the digital mission movement that would touch millions of souls.

As I sat on the edge of my couch, my wife asked me what the plan was. What was I going to do with One Voice? I began to cry.

"There's nothing to do," I said. "God is done with me. It has been a great run, but God must be done." As I sat there in tears, not acting in any way like the man of faith she had married, she spoke the following frightening words.

"I had a dream last night." Her dreams are terrifying because they are usually accurate.

With a nervous shake in my voice, I asked, "What did you dream about?"

She said, "I was in a room serving all these men. There was one man in the corner of the room weeping and looking as if he had been defeated. Then the late Reinhard Bonnke walked in. He walked around the room shouting with his strong German accent, 'Who is in charge here?'

"In the dream no one would reply. He asked again, 'Who is in charge here?' And with almost shame, all the men put their heads down and stayed silent. But on the floor was this man—weak, crying and lying prostrate on the floor. And with Bonnke's powerful voice that had preached to millions of souls, had cast out demons and had been used to raise the dead, he said to the man on the floor, 'Get up. You are in charge.' The man got up and instantly grew serious at Bonnke's declaration."

She said that she had woken up from the dream asking God what it meant. "When I came out here and saw you crying on the couch, I realized that the man in the dream was you."

She looked at me, with my eyes full of tears, and a small glint of hope began to flicker in my heart. Just as in the dream, she looked at me. With her firm, gentle voice, she spoke with the same authority as the German evangelist.

"Get up," she said. "You're in charge here. Lead again."

I knew in that moment the mission remained the same, but the method would have to change. The plan God had given me over a decade prior was still the plan He had. Youth were going to be saved all over the country, and God was going to use my life to do at least a small part of it.

The greatest pivot in my life and in the movement of One Voice was about to take place. The Lord was going to restructure completely how we reached youth to fit this generation in a way none of us could have foreseen.

I thought that God would use my life in a single, specific way to reach youth, but He had a very different plan. I would soon learn what the words "digital mission" and "digital missionary" would mean. I would soon discover a part of my calling that I never thought I would have. I would soon discover how God would take a company of missionaries to reach millions of people.

YOUR DIGITAL MISSION

Write down the Plan A you believe God has given you. What is the assignment He has placed on your life? Write it down on a physical piece of paper or in a note in your phone, hold it in your hand and pray the following prayer. Remember that faith comes through hearing, so while you are reading this out loud, receive faith for what God has spoken to you.

Jesus, I give You my Plan A. I also give You every other plan in my life. I may plan my ways, but You direct my steps. I trust You with my life. You have not led me wrong up to this point, and You will not start now. Take every bit of discouragement and turn it into faith. Take my weak yes, and may You change the lives of many people through that yes. In Jesus' name, Amen.

For training resources on this chapter's content, visit brian barcelona.com/dontscroll/.

When God Looks Different

As believers, we often anticipate how God will move in a current season based off the way He moved in a previous season. We look back at certain things He spoke to us, the music we listened to and the people with whom we hung out to determine how He will move now. These ideas can cause us to limit the way that God will move in our lives in the present season.

I always notice those moments in the Bible when it seems as if Jesus intentionally performed miracles differently than He had previously. I believe it was to show the disciples that there was not a formula to a miracle. Jesus showed up uniquely in every individual's life as they needed.

The common theme in every situation was the Kingdom of God advancing over the kingdom of darkness. But the way it happened in every individual's life was different. The woman with the issue of blood touched His clothes (see Mark 5:25–34). The Roman centurion received healing for his servant when he heard Jesus speaking a word (see Matthew 8:5–13). The blind man had Jesus' spit and mud wiped over his eyes and his vision was restored (see John 9:1–7). Jesus' methods always changed, but His mission remained the same.

God cares less about your method than He does about the mission He has given you. Let me start with one of the wildest disciples Jesus had: Peter. He was not put together, he made many mistakes, he spoke when he should have remained quiet and he was rebuked by Jesus. Yet this man carried a revelation that no one else had.

Jesus said that on Peter's revelation of who He was, He would build His Church (see Matthew 16:18). This was the man who brought a sword to the last prayer meeting Jesus had (see John 18:10). Let's put that in context in today's world. That would be like showing up to a prayer meeting with a gun. Logically, that does not make any sense.

> **God cares less about your method than He does about the mission He has given you.**

Peter always had preconceived notions of how Jesus would do things. I am pretty sure Peter thought the Messiah would at any moment say, "Now is the time to take up your arms. Let's overthrow that wicked Roman government."

I would like to imagine this was his motive for the sword. When the guards came to take Jesus, dressed in their armor in the shadow of night, he surely thought, *Now is the moment. I will defend this King Jesus with a method I know.*

45

As he swung the sword and cut off the ear of the guard, he probably waited for the smile and approval of Jesus for the action he had just taken. He probably hoped the next words out of Jesus' mouth would be, "It is time to take up arms and fight." But he did not find the reaction he was expecting. Jesus rebuked him instead, saying, "Put your sword back into its place; for all those who take up the sword will perish by the sword" (Matthew 26:52). Once again, Jesus dismantled Peter's method of thinking about how He should do things.

Without hesitation, Peter put the sword back, probably because the situation reminded him of the first time Jesus had changed His method and did things differently (see Luke 5). After disregarding the efforts of Peter and those who were with him, Jesus stepped into their boat uninvited and began to teach from it. He looked past the fact that they were probably frustrated at not being able to catch the fish they could have caught.

After He was done teaching, Jesus gave them a test to take—cast their nets. At the word of Jesus' instructions, a thousand thoughts probably crossed their minds: *We've done this before. Who is this rabbi to tell us how to fish?* But by blind obedience, these men followed His instructions. They threw their nets into the water, and the number of fish they caught astonished them.

Their obedience brought so much blessing that nearby friends had to come and help them. The boat they had used many times before began to sink under the weight of all the fish.

Can I relate this to you right now? As Jesus changes the methods and we obey blindly, the blessing that comes sometimes sinks the old structures, the old methods and the old ways we had used. When He changes the method, He forces us to embrace the new way that He wants us to do things. The mission stays the same, but the method changes.

See, Peter's mission remained the same. If you keep reading, you will see that Peter does not stop fishing, but Jesus changes what he fishes for. In the same passage, Jesus tells Peter, who has just embraced the fact that he was a sinful man and that Jesus is Lord, that he will now begin to fish for men (verse 10). Jesus was focused on Peter catching faith, not catching fish.

It is one thing to trust a method you have seen God use before. It is another thing to trust Him when He is doing something totally different. People who are resistant to change or to God shaking things up are people whose trust in Him has only been theoretical. They thought they trusted Him, but their trust had not moved from theory to reality. God changes things in their lives because He wants to give them an invitation to always follow a Man and not a method.

Maybe it is difficult for you to embrace the changes God has orchestrated in your life. That difficulty and struggle does not come because of the change in and of itself. The difficulty you are experiencing reveals that you have truly not been following Jesus, the Man.

The difficulty you are experiencing reveals that you have truly not been following Jesus, the Man.

This may be a harsh revelation, but it can change your life if you receive it with joy. This revelation is what changed my life. It is better to be shocked on this side of eternity than the other. Jesus had Peter do the most illogical thing you can think of—cast the nets again after they had finished fishing all night. His reason? To demonstrate that provision does not come from a method. It comes from Jesus Himself.

The year 2020 delivered me from my method and got me back on a journey of following the Man who saved my life. Most people who become jaded, wounded or offended by Christ put their trust initially in the method. You can see this with people who were hurt by the Church because they did not get a specific position they wanted, or they had expectations of leaders and pastors that those people could not meet.

See, they put their trust in the ways in which they thought God should move, whether it be in church buildings or ministry titles. So, when Jesus wants to do a new thing, it offends them. This is your opportunity. Press in and embrace the Man.

The greatest method that rocked the minds of the disciples was Jesus' death and resurrection. Think about this for a moment. Your leader, the Messiah, the One who heals the sick, raises the dead and casts out demons, is humiliated publicly and nailed to a cross. Talk about feeling disappointed.

His disciples must have felt great anguish, pain, confusion, fear and uncertainty. But the greatest thing I believe they struggled with was offense, because Jesus did not do what they thought He should have done. After all, He was God, right? He could have come down from that cross with twelve legions of angels at His disposal.

Yet what kept Him there was not nails or the weakness of His body. Think about this—death on a cross was not even His method. Jesus did not have this in mind. He even tried to change what He knew He had to endure by asking the Father to take the pain away from Him. Even so, Jesus trusted His Father more than He trusted His own method.

They brought the body of Jesus down from the cross—bloody, lifeless, the beginning stages of His wounds scabbing and drenched in sweat and blood from the trauma He had just endured—wrapped Him in a linen cloth and laid Him in a tomb. The hope of an overthrown Rome was gone. Most of the disciples went back to their original occupations. Some of them had scattered before His death at the sight of the soldiers in the Garden of Gethsemane.

Three days later, a few women wanted to bring spices for His body (see Luke 24:1). I think it is interesting that the women went. I am not quite sure if they had put their trust in what they thought Jesus should do as the men had. I would like to believe they just simply loved Him as a Man. As they found the tomb empty with the stone rolled away and encountered the angel, they knew in that moment that He had risen. But what would they do from there?

We read this story and think how cool that would have been to have seen this moment firsthand. Surely everyone would have been excited about the news of Jesus' empty tomb. But when I read this, I do not think that. I think, *Wow. No one is going to believe this encounter.* If I were these women, I would wonder what the disciples were going to say. They were experiencing such grief and disappointment since the method they thought Jesus would execute had not been realized. Now the women had to tell them that He was alive.

As they went back to the disciples, sharing all they had seen and heard, they should have experienced a moment of rejoicing, gladness and gratitude. That moment turned instead into a moment of doubt and unbelief.

"And when they heard that He was alive and had been seen by [Mary], they refused to believe it" (Mark 16:11). What a remarkable picture has been painted through those words. I want to pause a moment, because I think their refusal to believe came from a couple of different reasons.

The first is the question of why Jesus had not revealed Himself to them. Do we not all fall into this category at some point? We are offended because we did not get the revelation first. Even worse, people we deem to be "less than" us receive that great revelation.

The second reason is that maybe they did not understand what Jesus meant when He told them about His plan to suffer and be raised from the dead. Maybe He should have revealed to them how and when He was going to come back.

After their refusal to believe, Jesus appeared in a different form to two of the disciples while they were walking along their way to the country. They reported what they had seen and experienced to the others, but the others did not believe them, either (see Mark 16:12–13).

In this story in book of Mark, Jesus changed His form two times. The first form that He took was His renewed body, which He had revealed to the women at the tomb. When the men on the road would not believe, He graciously allowed Himself to take a second form in front of the two disciples. While He hoped to be recognized, He was once again met with their refusal to believe.

Understand that God is not boxed in by how we did things in years prior. If you are holding on to a past encounter that you have had with God, this expectation may be hindering you from seeing or understanding what He is asking you to do now.

God Is Revealing Himself in a New Way

I think it is so crazy that history repeats itself. We have heard that saying, and we have probably spoken that phrase ourselves. Let's now put it in modern-day context by going to the book of Malachi.

Although it takes you one second to turn the page from the end of the book of Malachi in the Old Testament to the beginning of Matthew, the first book in the New Testament, there were four hundred years of silence between Malachi and Matthew. During that time, God did not speak. I do not think He was silent because He did not care—I believe the silence came because God was giving an opportunity for people to seek His face and know Him by name.

But when that did not happen, God decided to make a triumphal entry. Instead of coming with lightning and thunder on a mountain as He did with Moses, He came representing Himself in a different way. He was not wrapped in smoke but wrapped in flesh. He dwelled in a manger that had been made by the hands of men.

Jesus stepped on the scene. God no longer wanted to be represented by mere prophets, so He sent the One who resembled Him most closely, His Son. Jesus began to share about His Father's Kingdom in ways no one had heard before. People were amazed at His teaching, because He delivered His message with authority (see Luke 4:32). Jesus decided that now was the time to reveal His Father in a whole new way.

This new method would not be based on how righteous the people thought they were or on how many Jewish laws they had to obey. Jesus took it a step further in Matthew 5 by caring not just for the external, but also for the hearts and motives of humankind. He touched the eyes of men.

As you continue to read through the New Testament, you can see that the message would go beyond the Jews, although they were a vital piece of the plan of God. He would also grace the Gentiles with the opportunity to hear the Gospel of the Kingdom.

I believe Jesus is doing something similar today. It seems as if the age we are living in could be a bit related to the end of the age of Malachi. We are witnessing things in this generation that could not have been fathomed in previous ones. Today, both you and I have the greatest privilege to either witness or be a part of Generation Z.

This generation, born between the years 1997–2015, has grown up in a largely post-Christian culture. Where there has been silence among Gen Z—the Word of the Lord is rare in their generation, since many do not go to church or have pastors in their lives—God has once again revealed His Son. Except this time, it was not in a manger. It was not through a church building. The creativity of God blows my mind because God chose to get to the heart of the next generation through their own eyes.

God knows that there is something they carry everywhere they go. It is a device that has been used for evil, for pornography, gossip and wounding others. This device, however, would become the very gateway for the Gospel of Jesus Christ to be made known among men and women. The cell phone, which has now become a common item among this generation, would become the donkey on which Jesus would ride into their lives.

For so many years, Christians have spent millions and millions of dollars building their ministries and putting higher education requirements on ministers. I am not saying that having a seminary degree is wrong, as I, myself, am furthering my own education in the Bible. What is wrong is disqualifying people we think are not smart enough. Because the last time I checked, Jesus did not pick smart people; He picked available ones.

Would it not be like God to make Himself known in Generation Z by speaking through Generation Z? And would it not be like God to use the modern-day technology to make His Son known among the nations?

Generation Z is one of the boldest generations I have witnessed. I have been able to watch firsthand the public transformation of the transmission of the Gospel from a wooden pulpit on a stage to a phone in a young person's hand.

God's heart for His Kingdom to be made known is so much more powerful than any method any of us could use. It just so happens that we who are alive today are witnessing the Great Commission being fulfilled digitally using social apps, livestream preaching, podcasts and YouTube videos. Christians have the ability to lift up their voices as never before. God is empowering everyday, ordinary people—not just experienced preachers. He is empowering the Body of Christ to live out the truth that we overcome by the blood of the Lamb and the word of our testimony. We do not love our lives, even unto death.

The rocks do not need to cry out. Instead, God is changing hearts of stone. God is saving drug addicts, kids with same-sex attraction or gender-identity confusion and people who are bound to addictions, and He is transforming them into

His greatest voices on the earth. The mission of the Gospel of the Kingdom remains the same, but the method has changed drastically. Digital platforms do not replace in-person interactions, but the ceiling we once had, the limitations we once had and the hindrances we once had no longer exist.

The age of digital missions has arrived. Does this not make sense when it comes to how Jesus said that every eye would see Him on that day (see Revelation 1:7)? He is washing away the borders of our countries and the limitations on the reach of our voices. And you who are reading this now have the opportunity to be on the forefront of what God is doing.

Yes, digital missions have their challenges. But does not everything else, too? I can imagine the very first missionaries who traveled outside the Mediterranean and the Middle East setting foot on new territory that was foreign to them, unsure of how to reach the people they were about to meet. They were unsure of the culture they were stepping into. But those brave missionaries, the ones who pioneered the Gospel in countries such as China, India and Brazil, did not let what was unknown stop them from preaching about the Man they did know.

The rules have changed. It is no longer the well-polished preachers we are looking for. We are not searching for the ones who have degrees and titles, although having those degrees with the proper heart does not hinder preaching. But find me the simple teenager who loves God and hates sin. Find me the faithful Christians who have been serving God for decades without a platform. Find me the mothers who have been raising their children with righteous values. Find me the youth pastor who has not had a big youth group or a large following but who has been faithful to his local church.

Those are the qualified.

Those are the ones who will be sent.

As Jesus once did after His resurrection, changing His form, He seems to be doing the same now. Maybe the form He is going to take today will look a lot like you sharing the Gospel through videos online. Remember, we are His hands and feet. His image is us.

Do not listen to those who tell you that you do not know enough. I have never met a person in my life who understood how his or her telephone microchips and towers work, but that has not kept people from receiving calls. I have never met a person who understood how every little electronic piece in his or her phone worked, yet that has never stopped millions from using their phones. Do not let what you do not know about the Bible stop you from using what you do know.

Do not do the devil's job for him. He is your accuser. Do not help him in his accusations.

Yes, there is always room to grow.

Yes, you must be fathered and mothered and keep older leaders in your life.

Yes, you must live a holy life and submit to the authority of God and to the authority figures. He has placed around you. But do not disqualify yourself. Do not do the devil's job for him. He is your accuser. Do not help him in his accusations.

Jesus Meets People Where They Are

Jesus had a lot of one-on-one encounters in the midst of the thousands who had gathered. You can see the uniqueness of the people He spoke with and how He always met people where they were. Whether it was Zacchaeus in a tree, the man bound in chains at the tomb or each disciple who encountered Him, Jesus had corporate messages that came packaged uniquely for every individual.

I have seen God do this on social media platforms like TikTok and Instagram, where people have come to faith by watching Gospel videos. We have seen atheists come to know the Lord. We have seen kids who have never stepped foot in a church watch our videos and receive Christ, join discipleship groups, get baptized and begin to share their faith—all digitally. I am a firm believer in discipling unto conversion.

The Bible is very clear as to how people are going to come to know Jesus. "How then are they to call on Him in whom they have not believed? How are they to believe in Him whom they have not heard? And how are they to hear without a preacher" (Romans 10:14).

Do you know whom this verse is talking about? It is talking about you! You are that preacher, the one who is called to share the news of the Gospel. You might have been called a lot of things in life by your family and friends, but today I want to call you a preacher and give you permission to preach.

Preachers are not just people who proclaim messages in churches or on street corners. They are not just people who are dressed in nice suits. Preachers are those who share the Good News of the Kingdom of God. The Good News that you were once lost and now are found, the Good News that you were once blind and now see. The Good News that there is a Kingdom that is greater than the kingdom of earth. It is a Kingdom that is not built by the hands of men.

The next wave of preachers will look far different from those in previous generations. They will care less about what kind of suits they have or what kind of cars they drive. They will, instead, care about how much time they have spent with God and how well they have loved people.

This next generation of preachers—you and your friends—will care less about how many times your name is plastered on a flyer or a screen. Instead, your greatest joy will be when His name is made known.

YOUR DIGITAL MISSION

Remember this: "As he thinks within himself, so he is" (Proverbs 23:7). How you see yourself in this season in which God may be doing something different will truly determine the fruit that is produced in your life. Pray this prayer with me:

Jesus, I accept my calling as a preacher of the Good News. My past, my economic status, my education, my age and everything else cannot prohibit me from sharing the Good News of what You did. Help me share Your Word with boldness. Let the love of God flow through my life. Give me great grace, and do not let the love of my heart grow cold. Let me embrace how You look in every season, even if it looks different from what I am expecting. In Jesus' name, Amen.

For training resources on this chapter's content, visit brian barcelona.com/dontscroll/.

Digital Missions

One hot summer day in Los Angeles, I got a phone call. I had been doing Instagram lives[1] with some of the most prominent, incredible faith leaders who love Jesus. Although these leadership talks were powerful and seemed to be successful at strengthening believers, I knew inwardly that we were not reaching youth as we could be.

I became discouraged when I wanted hundreds to join our social media live events but only ten would. I brought in the greatest voices I could think of: Todd White, Chandler Moore, Lou Engle, Dominic Russo, Nick Vujicic and Christine Caine, just to name a few. I even interviewed Jonathan Roumie, the actor who plays Jesus in *The Chosen* television show. Yet none of this was enough to see unsaved kids reached with the Gospel.

This left me frustrated. I was a preacher who had gone to high schools for over a decade, and now I could no longer preach in high schools due to the lockdown and pandemic of 2020. That hot summer day was interrupted by a phone call I received from my dear friend Aaron Custalow.

He said, "Brian, there was a word you received from God that said the One Voice Movement would lead to prayer being restored back to schools. Have you seen it yet? What are you doing with that word?"

I said, "I have not seen it, nor have I thought about it much."

"I believe I am to carry this word, then," Aaron said. "What if we do an event called *Gen Z for Jesus*, all digitally?"

At the first hearing of these words, I thought, *This event will never work. The name even sounds corny. But I trust Aaron and know that God is on his life.*

"If you will do it and you will lead it, we will back it," I replied.

"We have to do it on June seventeenth," he said. "That's the anniversary of when they removed God from public schools in America."

The only problem was that this conversation happened in May; therefore, we did not have much time to plan, organize and mobilize. For the next month, Aaron put together our team with his team in Virginia. To our surprise, when *Gen Z for Jesus* launched, 25,000 kids jumped on livestreams to pray, preach and share their faith. A hashtag we started reached millions of views in a matter of weeks. That event would be the match that sparked the digital mission movement in One Voice, which would lead to the digital Jesus Club movement that is now reaching millions.

That event would lead me to my burning bush experience; however, my burning bush experience would not be a burning bush that I would meet; it would be a burning man. His name was Gabe.

Two Teenagers

What you may not know is that One Voice Student Missions was birthed from a yes that started in my heart as a teenager. I responded to the Lord with a weak yes even when I did not know what the future would hold. But what has sustained One Voice, beyond the Lord, are the lives of the many high schoolers who have also said yes to God. From Jesus Club presidents to Jesus Club leaders, the kids I have reached over the last twelve years of my life have had a great impact on me.

This book would be incomplete without introducing you to the two teenagers who shaped what I believe will be the next decades of my life. God has a way of divinely interrupting men and women. And that interruption, if stewarded correctly, could become the greatest invitation to see great moves of God. That is exactly what happened in the summer of 2020.

Through a series of events and connecting points, I met a teenager who opened my eyes to the digital mission field. I learned very quickly that simplicity and authenticity far outweighed skilled preaching, big budgets and high production. That knowledge opened a door for me to be able to witness millions being reached with the Gospel.

God has a way of divinely interrupting men and women.

The humility that I needed to be able to receive from someone who was younger, and the courage it took for a teenager to teach someone who was older, would be the ingredients that were necessary to be successful in a digital mission movement.

Before I tell you the story of Gabe and his friend Mason, I want to set the stage for you to understand what digital missions are, why they are needed and why I believe they are the last line of defense against the spirit of this age. We always wondered how every eye would see, how every tongue would confess and how the Gospel reaching the world would hasten the return of Christ. Fifty years ago, no one could have imagined that the transportation of the Gospel would be through phones and apps, not just through planes, boats and cars.

The reality is that the harvest truly is plentiful and the laborers are few (see Matthew 9:37). The digital mission field now lies at our doorstep. This fact eliminates every excuse for you not to take the Gospel to your surroundings. And the digital mission field does not discriminate. Those who preach digitally are not required to be famous—only faithful.

Those who preach digitally carry a great weight on their shoulders to preach truth. As deception steers a generation away from God, those who preach the truth will see a generation set free. "You will know the truth, and the truth will set you free" (John 8:32).

This generation has no excuses as to why they will not share the Gospel. They cannot claim that there was not enough time, that they did not speak a particular language or that they had no means to share the message. The only reason why people young and old will not share the Gospel in the current decade will simply be because they did not want to.

Preparing the Way

Before the birth of Jesus, there was a woman named Elizabeth who carried a son named John, also known as John the Baptist. John the Baptist had one sole purpose: to prepare the way of the Lord. His message was simple, his method clear. He was a voice crying in the wilderness. "Prepare the way for the Lord" (Mark 1:3 NIV). As he was a voice for the first coming of Jesus, so this generation will be a voice for His Second Coming.

But before the Second Coming is to happen, people must hear of the first instance that Jesus arrived. This is where you play a role. The four hundred years of silence between Malachi and Matthew was broken with a crying baby. And although there was silence for four hundred years, there was a clue left in Malachi that ties the digital mission movement of today back to the Bible.

The clue was a verse you may have heard or read. "I am going to send you Elijah the prophet. . . . He will turn the hearts of the fathers back to their children and the hearts of the children to their fathers" (Malachi 4:5–6). In other words, someone would go before the Lord in the spirit and power of Elijah. The spirit and power of Elijah were for turning the hearts of the fathers toward the children and the disobedient toward the wisdom of the just, as is made clear in the Scripture verse. This makes a people ready and prepared for the Lord.

Let me break this down for you. God prepared the way for Jesus' first coming with a man who would walk in the spirit of Elijah. John's sole purpose was to turn the hearts of the fathers back to the children. You might think that is an easy task. But if it was so easy, our world would not be so broken.

The turning of a father's heart is a lot different from the turning of a father's discipline, words or opinion. You truly know we are in a revival when the fathers' hearts turn back to their children. I would argue that the greatest revival in history, beyond the explosion in the book of Acts, took place when Jesus walked the earth. There were so many miracles that they could not all be recorded. Yet the man who preceded that revival had this Malachi task: to turn the hearts of the fathers to the children.

I noticed in 2020 that the number of teenagers on social media platforms who were preaching the Gospel began to grow as never before. Seventeen-, eighteen-, and nineteen-year-olds grew platforms quickly with millions of followers. As I scrolled day after day, I wondered where the fathers were. I love when teenagers serve the Lord and preach the Gospel, but there is a level of depth and history that a father carries that a son does not.

For too long, fathers and mothers have felt irrelevant for the next generation. In the same way, sons and daughters have not understood the generational blessing of fathers and mothers. The digital mission movement has changed those rules.

If I could sum up the digital mission movement, I would describe it as a Malachi moment. The hearts of children are turning to the wisdom of the just. This is the first part. We have seen this in 2020. But now comes the second part.

The hearts of the fathers and mothers are needed in this last stand for this generation. What if the greatest invitation we could take is not just to some big platform at a church or conference, but rather meeting our youth on the front lines of where the war for their souls, minds and hearts is taking place?

Every group that is pushing demonic agendas understands that to reach a kid, you must meet them where they are. This generation of youth has been left to fight and fend for themselves for too long. In the midst of a hypersexualized culture, ideologies from hell, drugs, isolation, depression and suicide, the digital mission movement is calling fathers and mothers to stand alongside Gen Z and youth on the front lines again.

If you have phased out of ministry because of your age, you are being reenlisted. My prayer is that your hearts would turn back. Now let me jump back into my story of Gabe.

The hearts of the fathers and mothers are needed in this last stand for this generation.

Gabe Poirot was instrumental in introducing me to the possibilities of what we could see and do digitally. We talked for weeks, wondering if it might be possible to see digital missionaries preach the Gospel, win souls, disciple kids, baptize kids and see those kids commissioned as disciples.

As we dreamed for this, my heart grieved. I wondered where all the fathers and mothers in the faith who had made an impact on my life were. Did Gen Z even know them? Well, that desire of mine later played a role in these different ministries reaching youth. After weeks of talking with Gabe, I sat down with my team.

The COVID-19 season had discouraged me deeply. I felt as if a decade's worth of work that I had done for God had been smashed into pieces. With that mindset, I sat down with a few of my team members, some of whom were excited and some of whom said we would never make it on social media. To be honest, I was not even sure that it would work. But with a handful of people, we started *theJesusClubs* page on TikTok in July of 2020.

Without knowing it, Gabe and a handful of other Gen Zers were coaching, encouraging and in many ways discipling us on how to reach people digitally. We had our team all create accounts with the idea that the modern-day pulpits were our phones. One Voice and Jesus Clubs began to decentralize and empower voices—not people who were famous, because none of us were—and people who were faithful. It was not long before we began to see thousands follow our page and share our content. Not only that, but we watched as they were touched by God and found salvation.

Shortly after this, we launched our text number, which was a place where kids could message in questions or prayer requests or let us know that they wanted to give their lives to Christ. Our team would respond to these seven days a week as thousands of kids began to text in.

Prayer requests flooded our direct messages, or DMs. Questions about salvation and the end times, the mark of the beast and cultural issues began to pour in. Our following began to grow into the hundreds of thousands, and we were seeing our video views reach into the millions. God had taken twelve years of faithfulness and ripped open the curtain for the next generation to see. I began to realize that the rules had changed. What would have previously taken me a thousand years to accomplish was now possible with a handful of posts.

If you feel as if you have some importance in ministry or you have taken pride in your titles, understand that a terrible aspect of our culture is that we think we can only receive and grow from people who have done greater things than we have. We rarely look at someone's faithfulness as they journey day-to-day. We rarely care about someone's holiness. Sadly, in many ways, preaching has become a status game.

About this time, my wife and I flew to Dallas because we were getting ready to relocate. It was then that Gabe and Mason met me and my wife at a hotel and we began to make videos that spoke about Jesus. Mason Bristol was a friend of Gabe's who was also a teenager seeing millions of people reached with the Gospel.

In that hotel room, those two teenagers meant more to me than any megachurch pastor in the world. They did not have big names in the Church, they were not famous conference preachers, and they did not even have the latest brand of sneakers. But they loved God. And they were willing to do anything to reach people for Him.

As they walked me through how to post and edit videos to a greater level than I had formerly understood, it dawned on me that they were doing what the Holy Spirit had done in the book of Acts. They were teaching me the language of their generation.

I will be forever grateful for those two. They will always be heroes and legends in my heart. One day, when they get to heaven, I pray that they meet the millions of kids they had an impact on through those we have trained and will train across the globe.

History is rarely written by great people; it is written by simple people who did great things. The greatest thing those kids did that day was teach me to reach their generation. Gabe and Mason, my hat goes off to you guys. May you always stand and love God to the end of your days, and may we all hear, "Well done."

But it is not just them—you also have the ability to influence and share the Gospel.

A New Generation for Jesus

Many people have argued that we have to reach people Jesus' way. Typically, what that means to them is that we should resort back to the methods that Jesus used. I would highly disagree with that. It is actually impossible to reach people with the methods Jesus used, because I do not foresee anyone riding a donkey or walking from city to city with twelve people anymore.

We should recognize that methods change. The message and the mission will not change, but the methods used to convey the truths will. And that is what has happened in the last decade. Whether you realize it or not, we have shifted from only being able to share ideas with others in person to having at our disposal countless digital possibilities. God is entrusting us with both methods. We do not have to choose one or the other. We must steward our in-person life, character and calling, and we must also do that digitally.

A simple way of seeing your digital life and its impact is to look at it as similar to Peter's shadow. Peter's in-person method reached thousands. He healed the sick and probably cast out demons. But his shadow also carried authority and had the power to heal the sick (see Acts 5:15). God also gave Paul the power to perform unusual miracles—even handkerchiefs or aprons that he touched could be taken to the sick to heal them of a variety of illnesses (see Acts 19:11–12).

That is a picture of our digital presence. Our videos, just like Peter's shadow, can heal the sick. The comments that you type can change a life, just like the anointing left on a handkerchief. Take off your religious glasses for a moment and open your eyes. The message is the same. It is the same one that was shouted in the Bible; it is the same one that the demons shrieked: "Behold, the Lamb of God who takes away the sin of the world!" (John 1:29).

The message and the mission will not change, but the methods used to convey the truths will.

What once was shouted in Israel by one wild-looking man in the wilderness will now be shouted by millions across the globe. Jesus is worthy of every tribe and every tongue confessing He is Lord, and His worthiness and message can now reach the masses.

What a generation He has chosen to reveal Himself to in such a way! This is a generation that was born in technology. A generation whose attention, minds and hearts have been fought for by every major technology company. A generation that every group wants to manipulate and control. A generation that has grown up in a very different country than those before them. A generation of pandemics, economic crises and the uncertainty of the future. A generation of off-the-chart suicide rates and physical or emotional stress. Although this generation seems to be the most connected, they are also the loneliest, often mistaking followers and friend requests for true friends.

Oh, this generation. If you say it is one of the worst, lift up your eyes and see that this generation is not as it is because of its sin or even the sin of its parents. This is a John 9 generation. This is one that has been born blind to the truth. But its blindness is for one thing—that the works of God might be displayed. Gen Z could be the generation of the coming of the Lord or the true beginning of the birth pains. Who knows? One thing is for sure: Gen Z belongs to Jesus.

Gen Z is and will be the greatest proclaimers of the Gospel. Where previous generations have had great evangelists such as Billy Graham, Reinhard Bonnke and Louis Palou, Gen Z will not have a great evangelist in their generation. Gen Z *as a whole* will be the great evangelist.

Do Not Miss What God Is Doing Today

As you are reading this, I hope you see that language is beginning to form around what God is doing. I hope you now can see this is far bigger than a TikTok ministry page. This is far bigger than posting a video. God has ordained this moment and this time.

I have come to realize that sometimes God gives us eyes to see before He gives ears to hear. Sometimes the best thing to do when we do not understand what God is doing is not to say anything until it comes to pass. This is me telling you that it is coming to pass right now.

There are two types of people I have met who were alive during the Jesus movement. The first is those who tell all the stories of the Jesus movement and its greatness. They are the ones who talk about how salvation spread all over the nation and who remember what the Spirit of God did.

And then there are those who ask, "What Jesus movement?" They may have been Christians during that time and regularly attending church, but they were unaware of what God was doing.

Do not let that be you regarding what God is doing now. Do not let this move of God pass you by because you were stuck in what God used to do and not what He is currently doing.

When God Speaks, Go!

Have you ever noticed when reading the Bible that Jesus did not have a three-year ministry plan? His only plan was simply to obey what He heard the Father speak to him daily. Many times, what we plan can get in the way of the plans of God. Sometimes building out our yearlong schedule can put what we think God can or will do in a box. We justify our lack of faith or our inability to hear God daily by saying that we want to be "wise with our time."

But at what point does your faith end and your wisdom begin? At what point do your plans keep you from going where Jesus has called you to go?

I find it funny that we often worship and follow this Jewish carpenter only theoretically. To follow Him in reality can be very difficult for us. Nowhere in Scripture do you gather that Jesus had a routine or a schedule that He was not willing to disrupt. In fact, those around Him found it offensive that while He was on His way to where He wanted to go, He was sidelined by countless interruptions. Two such examples are the woman with the issue of blood (see Mark 5:25–34) and the blind man who screamed, "Son of David, have mercy on me" (Luke 18:39). Neither of those pauses in His journey were scheduled appointments; those were divine interruptions. The greatest form of obedience is to follow the voice of God and what He is telling you *today*, regardless of whether or not it follows your original plan.

Jesus' method of ministry was to do what He saw the Father do and to say what He heard the Father say (see John 5:19). That is what He taught His disciples. He also taught His disciples about the difference between recognizing the voice of God for their individual lives and responding to corporate commands, such as the Great Commission (see Matthew 28:18–20) and the Great Commandment (Matthew 22:36–38). With all my heart, I believe God is inviting us into the corporate message of preaching to youth and others who are in the digital space. This corporate message went out when Jesus said to make disciples (see Matthew 9:37–38), and nowhere did Jesus retract what He said.

So here you are, reading this book and hearing this story. What will you do? Will you say yes? Will you enlist in what God is doing today? Or will you hold on to what He did a decade ago?

YOUR DIGITAL MISSION

I hope you can see that what He is doing now is not different from what He was doing in the Bible. It is the same message but a different method. What do you do now?

Close your eyes and ask God to meet you. Ask Him for a burden and compassion for souls. And then ask Him how you are to answer that burden. Jesus had compassion for the lost and anointed His disciples to become answers to His prayer about sending laborers into the harvest. May you become the answer to Jesus' prayer and the prayer you are about to pray:

Jesus, give me a heart for Gen Z or whatever generation You want me to reach. Give me courage to speak truth in this generation. I enlist and reenlist in Your plans and purposes. Open my eyes to see the next steps I need to take. Take my life and write history with it. In Jesus' name, Amen.

For training resources on this chapter's content, visit brian barcelona.com/dontscroll/.

What Is the Gospel?

People rarely have a problem when you preach a gospel that will not ask them to give up anything. When they hear a gospel that says that they can make it to heaven and avoid hell by doing these little steps, or a gospel that says that Jesus went to the cross so that they do not have to, they have little resistance.

My prayer is that by the end of this chapter you will know what the Gospel really is, and if you have not yet, that you will pledge allegiance to Jesus. I pray that the Gospel you preach will be one that calls people to give their lives whole-heartedly to Christ with one hundred percent obedience to His Word.

Jesus invites each of us to embrace the cost of entering His Kingdom and to see it as a blessing and not a burden. Jesus is not as concerned as we are about our comfort level. He is concerned with our holiness. He wants us to know Him and make Him known.

Have you realized that every disciple died a horrible death of pain, shame and ridicule (except John the beloved, although he had his own share of suffering)? What drove them not only to die for the Good News but to live for it?

The disciples who died for Jesus did not die when they were killed physically. They had died to themselves a long time before. They knew that to gain their lives, they had to lose them. They followed Jesus daily, which allowed them to follow Him for a lifetime—even unto death.

My prayer is that by the end of this chapter you will know what the Gospel really is, and if you have not yet, that you will pledge allegiance to Jesus.

You will be persecuted, you will be mocked, you will be hated, you will not fit in and you will not be guaranteed to get rich. You may not be famous, you may be overlooked and unseen and you may be wounded by those you love. You will be reviled by many, you will be called to give up every right you thought you had and you will be told that your beliefs and the Book you follow makes others feel uncomfortable.

This is important for you to know as you begin to preach and reach this next generation. You can only outwardly call others to the message that you are living inwardly. Let this be an encouragement—Jesus' requirements do not lessen as generations go on. The same message that called Peter out of that boat and the same message that called Matthew out of the tax collector's booth is the same one that calls Gen Z to follow Jesus. And the Gospel they get saved to is the one that they will live out.

I want you to know what you signed up for when you chose to follow Christ. Jesus is our Lord and Savior, and Lordship is what separates the wheat from the chaff. Lordship is what allows those who follow Jesus to stand out from those who only claim to be Christian but who live lives totally opposite of God.

A prayer alone does not lead to a life with Christ. Just as faith without works is dead, your prayer is dead if it does not lead to life change. Jesus' Lordship must hold the same place in your heart as His role as Savior. Jesus saved you, and that salvation is the road for Him to become your King. He has a Kingdom and a way of life. Jesus is not going to rewrite those rules to lessen a struggle we have that is hard to overcome or so that we can fit into the current culture.

Just because you cannot accept the fact that this loving God would have us change something in our lives in obedience to His Word does not mean that is not His nature.

Growing up as a millennial in the generation of participation awards, it was hard for me to hear correction or see that there were winners and losers. But the truth is that there are winners and losers in both the Kingdom and in the Bible. There are those who make it and those who do not.

The Bible is always relevant, even when cultures, nations and leaders say it is outdated. The freedom we are looking for in Jesus is going to come when we embrace this Gospel, this Good News that Jesus brings. Our lives will never change when we try to bend God's Word to fit our narrative. A Gospel that is preached inaccurately will keep producing a powerless Christianity. A Gospel that does not have fruit will be good for nothing. A fruit tree that bears no fruit is worthless. So is our Christianity when it does not produce the fruit of the Spirit.

Just know that people will not have any issues with what you say as long as the message that you share fits into their daily lives. They will not argue with a faith that acts like an accessory that they add to their outfit without challenging anything about their way of life. Again, this may sound repetitive, but you must get this in your DNA. You must not be afraid to call the next generation to wholehearted obedience to Christ.

What we have found to be the most received message of Gen Z is an unadulterated, uncompromising Gospel with power that is followed by signs and wonders. This is your permission to preach the truth in love to see Gen Z and the generations that follow know Jesus.

It amazes me that for so many years Christians have tried to take the name of Jesus out of their music, their social media and their events, hoping to sneak attack the Gospel into culture. That is why I loved when Kanye West came out with his ninth album in 2019. He was a man who was not a pastor and who had no lifestyle of living for Christ, but he was bold enough to call his chart-topping album *Jesus Is King*. If Kanye was not ashamed to tell the truth, we should not be either.

Although the Gospel is free to receive, it will cost you everything to live. When we proclaim Jesus as Lord and Savior, the Gospel becomes our new life. Our old way of thinking dies, the eyes through which we see life are redeemed, and we can now see life and God through grace and salvation. This new light allows us to live differently.

Do you see how this changes the way you see the prayer you prayed to ask Jesus into your heart? Can you see how that moment was the beginning of a covenant that would last a lifetime? Can you see it had a far deeper meaning than just a reaction to a message you heard years ago from a preacher who had you respond to an altar call?

Do you also see that as you begin to preach both digitally and in person, this changes the conviction from which you preach? If the end goal of your message or video is for someone to merely say a prayer, you have missed the real objective.

Every word you say as you share the Gospel digitally matters. One teenager could be watching that video, and the message you are speaking may be a seed that is being planted, or it may even turn into the moment when they accept Christ. That is why it is so important to make the cost of following Jesus very clear to the people with whom you talk. To pray a prayer of salvation after hearing the Gospel presented but live no differently going forward is like getting married but continuing to live as if you are single. Doing so would make no sense, because marriage is not an event, it is a lifestyle. From the moment you say, "I do," marriage requires a totally different way of living.

Yes, that is how fast it happens. You are still single the second before that simple "I do." The moment you say it, however, you are married. And when you get married, everything changes. You change your bank accounts to combine your finances, you have to consider the other person as you both live under one roof, your good habits should grow and your bad habits have to change. In most situations, women change their last name from the one they inherited from their family to the last name of their spouse. Why? Because the covenant demands a lifestyle change.

77

That is also how quickly we go from the kingdom of darkness into the Kingdom of light. Within seconds, His Kingdom changes everything. Just as with marriage and how the covenant you entered makes you no longer a lone individual, when you accept Jesus and live the Gospel, you are no longer alone. You have entered into a covenant. As your mind begins to embrace this, you can begin to see how living the Gospel is good. It is vital that we share the faith into which we got saved with others.

That is also how quickly we go from the kingdom of darkness into the Kingdom of light. Within seconds, His Kingdom changes everything.

If we do not live in this way, it does not only damage us and our faith, but we validate the hypocrisy that has driven so many away from God. It is one thing to know what we got saved from, but it is another to know what we were saved for. Do you know what you were saved to do? We all have things that Jesus set us free *from*. Maybe for you it was loneliness, self-hatred, suicide or a broken heart. Those are the things that Jesus saved you from. What He saved you *to* is a new way of living. You were saved so that your life would now have an impact on others as you bring Jesus to those around you.

Every time you share the Good News of Jesus, you are encouraged to share about how you received a changed life, one that this next generation could have. Following Jesus is trading our mourning for joy, our addiction for freedom and our selfishness for selflessness. It is knowing that there is real freedom in Christ. Minds can be renewed, and our feelings and emotions can be submitted to Jesus.

You have been called to preach and disciple one of the wildest generations. What does that say about you and how God sees you? You may feel unqualified and not equipped, but God equips those He calls. Many are called and few are chosen, because few choose the call.

As a believer, you know that the Gospel is the greatest invitation and interruption of your life. It asks you to lay down every right you think you have. With great joy, you will be seen by many as foolish. We forsake our lives and loved ones for the sake of the Kingdom, not loving anyone above Jesus. We know that our greatest reward lies beyond this earth, and our inheritance is God. It is the greatest legacy we can leave.

We must remember the Kingdom of God is one that looks nothing like anything we have ever known before. To be seen we must hide, to be heard we must whisper and to be rewarded we must do good things in secret.

You may be thinking, *How will I live this? How is it possible to give up everything? How do I truly make Jesus my everything? How do I lay my life down?* The answer is quite simple. We have often complicated it because it is so simple. The Bible is heaven's manual on how to live for God, and it is the Good News of the Kingdom.

Do you realize that the fact that there is another way of living life is good news? We are not bound to our sinful nature, or worse, our dead religion. We have access to finding life. But that access only comes when we lay our lives down. It comes in giving up ourselves as a living sacrifice (see Romans 12:1). The Bible calls it denying ourselves (see Matthew 16:24). But the only way we can live this out is to understand that God is not asking you to do something He has not already done.

There is a reason why Jesus says, "Blessed is any person who does not take offense at Me" (Matthew 11:6). The offense comes when you worry and agonize over what you will lose if you live a Christianity as the one I am describing. But if that is your thought, you have it backward. It is not what you lose; it is what you gain. Jesus is able to ask people to lay down their lives only because He has a better one to give. He knows that you and I could not have both the old and the new.

A lot of this information may be familiar to you. If that is the case, my hope is that this explanation will take truths that you have had in your head and drive them into your heart. From out of your heart is where you will need to preach to reach Gen Z. They will connect with the message coming from someone who has a sold-out heart and who loves God. They will not as easily connect with someone who just has head knowledge of God.

The Gospel of the Kingdom

I believe one of the greatest messages Jesus preached about the Kingdom is found in Matthew 5. It gives an incredible outline of how to explain the cost of the Gospel. This biblical passage will be key as you preach to this next generation. You can see this chapter through two different narratives. The first is that you can see the hardships we are called to face as believers. The second is that you can see that every opportunity we have to deny ourselves and our selfish desires is a yes to God and a yes to the Gospel.

Here is the first way to see this. Jesus calls us to be poor in spirit, which does not seem like anything we would want to be. He calls us to mourn, and He calls us to be meek even when we think we need to be powerful. He calls us to be hungry and thirsty for righteousness instead of being satisfied, and He calls us to give mercy in order for us to receive mercy.

He calls us to be pure in heart. In the Greek language, the word for heart is *kardia*, which means "purity in our thoughts and emotions."[1] Jesus calls us to bring peace when we have not done anything wrong. He tells us we are going to be persecuted, but He never gives us permission to defend ourselves. Jesus even tells us we will be insulted and falsely accused, but He does not give us permission to lash out or point out the mistakes of our accusers.

In no way with my natural eyes and understanding does this seem like anything I would want to do, let alone think that God's Kingdom is a good fit for me. This perspective on Jesus' calling for our lives only changes when my eyes and heart see and understand through the Gospel. Although it can seem as if we are losing much, let me point out what we gain.

This gain in Christ will be the turning point for this next generation. Gen Z has grown up in a generation of bad news. They see the Bible as a book that culture has twisted. We must show them the joy that is found in laying down our lives. In order for us to show them the joy, however, we must first carry the joy. Joy is different from happiness. Happiness is an emotion, while joy is a state of being. It is who we are. As Gen Z has been plagued with depression, suicide and mental health issues, they need to see that the joy of the Lord will be their strength.

Using the passage in Matthew 5, let's look at all that we gain as believers. Let's see the joy that is found in Christ, and let this be the foundation from which we will preach. Look at this. We are promised:

- the Kingdom of heaven
- to be comforted and never left alone
- to inherit the earth
- to be satisfied
- to receive mercy
- to see God
- to be called sons—inheritors—of God
- the Kingdom of heaven now for the second time
- a reward in heaven

What incredible gifts! Too many times I have been guilty of only wanting to share with someone what God will give them but not the price they will pay. I have failed many times to communicate the great exchange the Gospel gives us.

Lately, I have wondered if all those years that I preached if my message was this clear. Did people leave feeling as if they followed God, or did they leave feeling as if God would follow them?

Everything I have written prior was to get you to this point. The clear message of Jesus is the only thing that will save this generation. The great exodus of our faith in this age seems not to be the denial of Christ, but rather those who thought they were following Jesus but never were.

The clear message of Jesus is the only thing that will save this generation.

We were never meant to *sell* the Gospel. We were meant to *tell* the

Gospel. When you sell something, you have to hype it up to get the consumer to buy it. But Jesus is not looking for consumers. He looks for those who would be consumed—consumed by God and His calling. He is looking for men and women who would be sold out for the King.

Gen Z is not interested in flashy lights or a well-known speaker. This generation wants truth, justice and a cause that they can live and die for. Jesus Christ is the only One who can fulfill those longings of the heart and soul.

Joy in Living the Gospel

As I have shared on what the Gospel is and how to live it, there is one more vital component you must understand. Without this point, your efforts would simply be religious.

Say this with me out loud: there is great joy in living the Gospel.

Say it again! There is great joy in living the Gospel.

Say it again and again until your heart believes it. Write it on a piece of paper, and stick it to your bathroom mirror if you have to. There is great joy in living the Gospel.

Joyful preachers are those who will emerge in this generation. There will be those who will continue to allow the Gospel to form and reform current beliefs and lead to all emotions. We will not fall into the trap of what culture wants to push us into. As the world screams one thing, we will shout another. From the rooftops to the churches to our neighborhoods and to the internet, we will proclaim, "There is a joy in living the Gospel."

We know that the Kingdom of God is to be our final destination. Jesus' ability to heal the sick was easy for Him, because the Kingdom He was from had no sickness. Loving the broken was easy, because the One on the throne is full of mercy that is new every morning.

Jesus lived the Gospel of the Kingdom, because He witnessed it firsthand. The cross could be endured by Him, because the redemption of humanity was the joy set before Him. I can imagine Jesus thinking, as He was beaten, bruised, bleeding, in pain and hanging on the cross, "My Kingdom is so wonderful that I want them to get a taste of it on the earth and to experience its fullness when they die. I will make a way for them to have access forever."

I have recently seen many Christians falling away from the faith in the name of deconstruction and enlightenment. I have heard them saying that the hurt and pain they experienced in the Church has caused them to leave. They say they love God, but they do not think the rules and teachings of Jesus bring freedom. They say God's laws are bondage and dangerous, some calling the cost we are to pay for following Christ a burden. They do not revere God's Word as the ultimate authority. This is the demise of their so-called faith.

This kind of teaching wants the promise without the price—like having sex without marriage. That kind of Gospel will lead your faith to death. And God does not work that way. His Kingdom will challenge your culture and your norms. His Kingdom will confront the areas of your life that do not align with His commands.

We must be careful not to bite the fruit of the culture or run to what sounds appealing. When you enter this walk with Jesus, you will experience many challenges. You will need to lay your life down continually. Yes, you will live for God, which means that you will die daily.

The Gospel will offend us, because the Gospel is not about us. This is why Progressive Christianity is not Christianity at all.[2] This may be the first time you are hearing the term "Progressive Christianity," but it will not be the last. Progressive Christianity is running rampant in Gen Z as false teachers preach from their unhealed wounds and their offense with the Church.

All that I have said about sacrifice is critical, because the pitfall of progressive preaching is so deep. Those who are preaching Progressive Christianity have teachings that are centered around how you feel and what version of God you want to serve. The justification of sin only amplifies what spirit is behind that message. This is why I said that if great numbers fall away from Christ, it will not be those who are denying Jesus, but rather those who thought they were saved but were not.

Remember that the Kingdom of God is not a democracy; it is a theocracy. We do not vote, and we do not have rights. Instead, we have a King, a great and perfect leader named Jesus, and we obey His commands because we love Him. "Blessed is any person who does not take offense at Me" (Matthew 11:6). This statement from Jesus came at a time when John was asking his disciples if Jesus was the Messiah; therefore, Jesus began to state all the works He was doing.

"The blind receive sight, the lame walk, those who have leprosy are cleansed, the deaf hear, the dead are raised, and the good news is proclaimed to the poor" (Matthew 11:5 NIV). This was foreign to those who followed God back then.

Similarly, will we be offended when Jesus moves in ways we thought He would not? Now more than ever, we must remain purehearted and know that our generation is responsible to tell those who follow us about the works of God (see Psalm 145:4). The message we share will guide them, but the message we live will shape their faith!

That clear message will either set up the next generation for success or for the death of their faith. But a watered-down message—a Gospel that says God wants to only give to you and the requirement from you is minimal—is why we have the teachings we do today. What one generation had in moderation, the next has in excess.

The message we share will guide them, but the message we live will shape their faith!

This could not be truer now. The self-centered worship songs and messages over the last twenty years have pushed this generation further from God than ever before. At the same time, it has produced a desire for the real thing. Gen Z sees past the big screens, fog machines and over-rehearsed worship sets. It sees past our polished messages into what truly lies within. There is a demand on millennials and previous generations to live authentically. They are to lead from love and to give grace to this next generation as they journey to follow God.

The wonderful thing about this is that Christ has already prepared Gen Z to receive the truth about how to live joyfully with Him! Many have become disillusioned with the falseness of the current culture. We can see this in the anti-pornography movements, a distaste for hyper sexualization, a pushback against the need to project fake personas on social media, a hatred for injustice and a desire to do something meaningful in the world.

Previous generations have placed a huge emphasis on going to church, tithing, raising money for building projects and caring more about how everything appeared on the outside than the inside. When I was growing up, church attendance was much more important than inward discipleship, and I knew this because my grandma, who was one of the few believers in my family, talked less about the transformation of the Gospel than about going to church. I do not think her heart was bad. I just think that is what that generation was taught. They were taught that location equals transformation, which is far from the truth.

But not every church operated this way, and the hearts of many pastors and leaders were not necessarily in a bad place. The church just did what we knew to do; therefore, an overemphasis on Sunday mornings became the prime center of our faith. We missed Monday through Saturday. While we centered youth outreach around a Wednesday or Friday night, we missed what it would look like to have a connection with them on a daily basis. This is where the digital space changes that.

What prior generations should have given us was not Guitar Hero, youth group games, movie nights, video games or pointless messages of motivation that only excited us for a moment. Those things are not sinful, but none of them prepared us for the life Jesus calls us to live.

We need to be taught how to die daily, how to live holy through loving God and how to do our works in secret to gain rewards in heaven.

We need to be taught the importance of the Old Testament and how vital Israel is to the plan of God.

We need to be taught about the end times and how we are to prepare for the persecution that lies ahead.

We need to let people know from the very beginning what they are saying yes to. We have a responsibility to prep them for the times that are to come. They will give an account for their faith, but we will give an account for how we stewarded the next generation.

What I remember when I was younger was how most messages centered around the audience with preachers trying to keep people saved. It was almost as if the generation before mine was scared to call my generation to sell out for God because they were not sure how we would take it. Ultimately, this method came from a lack of hunger and pursuit of God from previous generations. It came from thinking that if we looked like the world, we could lead the world to Christ, but that method was never in the Bible.

Jesus disrupted both cultural and religious norms. At the same time, He always honored the law by fulfilling it instead of abandoning it. Now more than ever, we must allow God to work in and through us instead of abandoning His ways. Those who follow us will have a chance to live out radical faith—which should not really be that radical. If Christians live out what the Bible instructs, that is normal faith. When Jesus called us to make disciples (see Matthew 28:18–20), He was not asking for a favor. He was giving a command. It is our time to rise up and joyfully live out that call.

The Gospel of Following Jesus Daily

What if the method of disciple-making that we have been doing has not been reaching its fullness? What if our over-emphasis on a prayer or on hands being raised at a service has hindered the greatest invitation of following Jesus? What if this is why Jesus did not tell His disciples to accept Him, but instead told them to *follow* Him?

Accepting is a lot easier than following, because accepting something can be momentary, but following is daily. Western culture tells us to accept everything and everyone just as they are. But acceptance rarely leads to change. You can accept that Jesus is Lord, and you can accept that He is the Savior, but that is very different from following or living those words.

Jesus' disciples followed Him long before they received Him. I know this is going to go against your Western Church mindset, but think about it with me for a minute. He taught them how to cast demons out, heal the sick and raise the dead long before He made them temples of the Holy Spirit. Jesus had not died yet, so—according to our definition of how salvation took place through the death of Jesus—they were not saved yet. They were, nevertheless, doing the work of God. I think Jesus knew that if the disciples were able to taste and see that He was good, they would never need to be convinced or seduced to follow Him. Their natural eyes saw the Gospel being lived out, and that was enough.

It was December of 2020. I had preached the New Year's Eve service at my home church, UpperRoom Dallas. As I shared all that God had done in my life and in the lives of my friends and family, I finished by inviting people to follow Jesus. I did an altar call as I had done so many other times in my life. Young people, adults and kids came forward to receive Christ.

Near the end of the service, a young man who had grown up Buddhist came to me with a question I had never heard before.

With sincerity and love, he said to me, "I don't know if I'm ready to accept Christ. Will I go to hell if I don't pray a prayer tonight?" I stood there astonished that this was the first time in twelve years of preaching I had ever heard this question.

I looked at him and said, "Look. There are times when people like me walk into a church and receive Jesus. There are other times when people take a little longer to get to know the Man they are going to give their life to. If you are on the journey of wanting to get to know God, stay on it."

You may ask, "What about praying the prayer of salvation?" That question is why we have powerless churches and powerless Christians who have a powerless Gospel. We have settled for hands raised and not changed lives. We have settled for feeling good at the end of a night of preaching by measuring the response to an altar call without following up with those who responded. We have settled for packed altars but not new hearts. God can and has worked in altar calls all over the world, but we need to continue to be in contact with those people after their initial response to the Gospel. We need to step into others' lives and walk with them actively, as Christ did with His disciples.

Living the Gospel

I cannot tell you how many times I have had to ask the Lord to forgive me for not living the Gospel of the Kingdom. At times, I have even been afraid to call people to an all-in lifestyle of following God in fear that the message would seem too much, or that following Jesus would seem too burdensome. As I stated before, this is not true. Wherever you are at, will you pray with me?

Jesus, thank You for revealing truth to our hearts. Thank You that the Good News of the Kingdom is possible to know and live out. Thank You for the grace and mercy You give us every day. Thank You that we still have time to know You and make You known. Forgive me for times when I have seen Your ways as a burden, for times when I have chosen not to live out the Gospel and for times when I felt I knew a better way. Forgive me for being offended with Your leadership and thinking I know better than You. Give me humility and a heart to obey. Your ways are higher than mine, and I trust Your leadership. Keep me from deception, and keep my reward of You, Jesus, at the forefront of my mind. Help me to preach truth to the next generation and to bless Israel. In Jesus' name, Amen.

YOUR DIGITAL MISSION

Although the following items can be a part of sharing the Gospel, these things are not necessarily the Gospel in its entirety.

- Sharing prophetic words
- Amazing worship moments
- Telling someone God loves them
- Praying for someone to get healed
- Reading a Bible verse

Remember, the Good News—which is the Gospel—that Jesus and the apostles shared was about another Kingdom that would come. What gave access to that Kingdom was the acceptance of the Savior, who gave His life to pardon our sins.

I encourage you to share about the Kingdom of God. Tell others about how it is shown partially in the day in which we live, and how it will be fully manifested when Christ comes back. See the Appendix: How to Lead Someone to Christ at the back of this book. It provides important elements and suggestions to include in your Gospel presentation.

For training resources on this chapter's content, visit brian barcelona.com/dontscroll/.

Long-Term Evangelism

As I mentioned in the previous chapter, New Year's Eve 2020 had been a powerful night. I had preached at UpperRoom Dallas's New Year's Eve service, and many had given their lives to Christ. Like most services, there were a handful of people who wanted to meet me and talk to me after my message. But one person in particular stood out to me. He did not come with the usual handshake or request for a picture. This young man came with a question I had not heard in all the years I had followed God. If he had asked me the question only a few months earlier, I would have had a different response.

As I mentioned earlier, with deep sincerity this young man said, "I'm not sure if I fully believe what you are saying, but what I am sure of is this—I know that Buddhism, the religion of my family, is fake. I'm starting to believe the words you're saying about Jesus, but I still want to get to know Him. Will I go to hell if I don't pray a prayer tonight?"

This question was powerful to me for a few reasons. The first was that he expressed that he knew that Buddhism was a false religion. The second was that even before accepting Christ into his heart, he was feeling the tug of God drawing him near, something that only the Holy Spirit can do. This caused me to look deeper into his question. I took my eyes off what would have been the expected response in Western Christianity—encouraging him to pray the sinner's prayer immediately—and reminded myself of how God uniquely draws individuals.

I told him what a powerful question he had posed. Although it was not one that I could answer with wit or a joke, I paused, smiled and chuckled a little bit as I thought, *Wow. This is profound.*

I began to explain to the young man that according to the Bible, Jesus' disciples did not accept Him or confess Him as Lord during their first encounter with Him. They never prayed a prayer. Jesus did not give a compelling message to get them to sign up for His ministry, nor was He trying to pack out altars for a good picture for the next promo. In fact, what He told them was probably vague to them. His "altar call" moments were summed up in two words: follow Me. But with those words, the early disciples began a journey of following Him to get to know Him and to truly give their lives to be His disciples.

"Let's take Peter, for example," I told the young man. "He is one of my favorite disciples in the Bible. He was a man who did not receive the revelation of who Jesus was when he first met Him. After Peter had walked with Jesus for a season, he confessed Him as Lord. He even ended up meeting his death by hanging upside down on a cross because he was a follower of Him. Peter began a journey with Jesus and followed Him until his absolute conversion and devotion."

But here is the hard thing to wrap our minds around, and this question and its difficult answer not only applies to the lives of the disciples but also to those of us living in the digital space today. When does conversion happen?

Did Peter's conversion happen the moment he followed Jesus, or could his response to Jesus have been simple curiosity? Did his conversion take place the moment he walked on water, or could that have been him testing to see if Jesus truly was the Messiah? Maybe his conversion happened the moment he said, "You are the Christ." Have you ever thought of that? And does that mean the moment he denied Jesus that he left his faith, or, as some would sadly believe, does it mean that he was never saved at all?

The Bible does not lay out the exact moment each of the disciples' hearts came into the belief that Jesus truly was the Son of God. But it does lay out their journey and the life they lived that showed their devotion.

You may never know which of the many hundreds of videos a kid watched was the one that had an impact on him and led him to make the decision to follow Jesus. And as I continue, my heart is that you would have eyes to see beyond a hand raised or a prayer prayed. To do that, you must take your eyes off what is seen and focus on

I pray that you would celebrate the journey people go on to discover that Jesus truly is the Son of God and that He is worthy of a lifetime of devotion.

what God is doing behind the scenes. I pray that you would celebrate the journey people go on to discover that Jesus truly is the Son of God and that He is worthy of a lifetime of devotion.

Back to the story. I asked the young man if he knew what a shotgun wedding was. He said no.

I said, "A shotgun wedding is when two people get married in the spur of the moment. The reason they call it a shotgun wedding is because the man has to fear the father of the woman coming out with a shotgun." We both laughed.

I said, "There are some conversions to Christ that are like shotgun weddings. At the moment someone hears of the Good News of Jesus, they immediately accept and immediately follow. There are plenty of shotgun weddings that actually turn into great marriages, but there are also shotgun weddings that don't end so well."

As I gave this explanation, I could tell that he began to think and ponder if he wanted a shotgun wedding with Jesus or if he was going to take a little bit more time to get to know Him.

There are people who accept Christ with great excitement and emotion, but they do not fully know what they said yes to. We see this in the parable of the sower (see Matthew 13). In this parable, Jesus explains that there are four types of soil. He spoke about the rocks that represent the people who receive Jesus with joy, but because they have no roots, their devotion to God is only a temporary, emotional experience. This is so prevalent in today's culture, as emotion-driven Christianity is what most people have accepted.

He also spoke about those who are like the road that leaves the seeds exposed to the birds. In this scenario, the devil comes with lies and deceit, taking away the truth that God deposited in the soil. This is why digital missions is important. As we create daily content that is centered around Jesus, we are redepositing truth back into the minds of a generation that is being attacked by a devil who is trying to snatch the Word away. We are continuing to water on a daily basis those seeds that have been planted.

The Bible also speaks of the good soil. This soil represents those who understand the Word and faithfully live it out. The seed that falls on the good soil bears fruit and brings forth an immense crop.

The soil I saved purposefully for last is the soil that has thorns. The Bible says it represents the man who hears the truth, but the worries of the world and the deceitfulness of wealth choke the Word. This happens to the point that the man becomes unfruitful to it.

If something becomes unfruitful, at one point it had been fruitful and borne fruit. Too many people fall into this category. They were once Christians, but now they are not. Their lives once bore the fruit of Christ, but they bear nothing now. For some, this happens due to the events of life. For others, it happens because of the lack of stewardship in their walk with God.

Like any garden that is unattended, it will grow thorns and weeds, which come up and choke out the life of what is intended to be growing. And whether your life stops bearing fruit because of things that have happened to you or because of your personal choices, the result is the same: you stopped bearing fruit. If your soil is no longer bearing fruit, I encourage you to water it, clear the weeds and the thorns and wait to see what God will grow in the soil of faith.

How do we change the trajectory of young believers and help them bear fruit for their entire lives? We do what Jesus did. We live our lives fully for God, we preach the Word and we change the way we see evangelism. It should not be a momentary event, but rather a lifelong process of teaching someone how to follow Christ. For too long, we have tried to microwave the process of someone accepting Christ. There must be an urgency to preaching the Gospel of Jesus, but everybody is different.

That is why I told the young man, "I believe that your heart is sincere, and I believe you want to get to know who Jesus is. You long to follow Him. It seems like you also want to watch what He can do in your life before you fully make that commitment to be one of His disciples. To me, you are no different from one of the disciples in the Bible. And your journey is just as valid as the ones who came up to pray a prayer tonight."

Teenagers to Martyrs

The term *long-term evangelism* does not mean taking a long time to lead someone to Christ. It is understanding that people have different time lines and processes. Whereas one person may hear or read the Bible and understand it all right away, others may take time to understand and obey the Word fully. They need time to grow in deep relationship with God, and they need time to deny themselves, pick up their cross and follow Jesus.

I was given a Bible when I got saved. I read it and immediately understood it. I am not saying I believed it all. I remember being seventeen, sitting at my kitchen table and reading verses about how Jesus healed people. I kept telling Him, "I don't believe this. I don't believe that You healed the blind, and I don't believe You raised the dead. But help my unbelief."

And He did.

Many in the Church have compromised what authentically following Jesus means simply to see more hands raised in a service. To make our egos feel good, we have settled with exaggerated numbers without seeing real fruit in the Kingdom of God. Most of us are guilty of this. After all, it feels good to say that one hundred people accepted Christ. I have observed that although we are never to judge if people have or have not authentically received Christ into their lives, the message they heard when they got saved is the one that will be lived through their lives.

I find it ironic that Jesus chose a method of soul winning that is rarely used today. Instead of inviting people to an altar, He invited them on a journey. Instead of focusing on their outward sin, He went after their hearts. Instead of choosing to be loved by the religious leaders, He chose to sit among those who were broken. He did not disqualify people from ministry even though He could see their many character deficiencies. This made His message less about their outward performance and more about their inward heart.

Everything about Jesus' life was different. He chose to invite people on a journey to both hear of and witness the Kingdom of God. Jesus knew that more would be accomplished through the disciples if they spent three years seeing Him live the Kingdom of God than if they spent thirty years talking about the Kingdom of God.

Do you see the significance of the digital space? As youth see the miracles of God, the salvation of God and the power of God daily, they will want to know this God we serve. God will transform Gen Z from being teenagers to martyrs, just as the disciples were transformed after they walked with Jesus.

"Faith comes from hearing, and hearing by the word of Christ" (Romans 10:17). I believe that we have limited how we hear the Word of Christ to church services and outreaches. We should realize that the loudest and most influential voice is the person who wholeheartedly practices what he or she preaches. Why do most of us respect our grandmothers and grandfathers? Because time after time, we have seen that generation live consistently.

It is time we do the same with our faith. It is time that our prayer meetings become a prayer culture. It is time that church is no longer something that is just attended, but it is what we belong to. It is time that—regardless of what we feel—our faith triumphs.

Slow Down Your Evangelism

Over twelve years, I have preached the Gospel to thousands of people. In this last season through the digital space, I have preached to millions. If there is one thing that I want you to take away, it is that there is an urgency. Souls must be saved, demons must be cast out and the sick must be healed. But as we look at Jesus, we see that He was never in a rush.

Even though the Bible says that not even the libraries of the world could contain the number of Jesus' miracles (see John 21:25), you never see Jesus being hasty. Nowhere do you see Him upset at all the interruptions that took place. Long-term evangelism is exactly that. There is an end goal of souls being saved, but there is a slowing down and stopping for the one. There is an understanding that God cares uniquely about every individual's life, and He gives them precisely what they need when they need it.

The greatest disciples are not made in a five-minute altar call. They are made through relational investment and discipleship. My wife and I have poured into many people's lives over the years. It is funny how discipleship works. There are times that I have invested in individuals for many years regarding a specific struggle, but I do not seem to see any progress. Yet one day, they wake up and realize they do not have that struggle anymore. That is one of the greatest rewards of those who disciple. The reward of discipleship is not better workers for our ministries, but people who love God and obey God more. This love and obedience will lead to a life that has an impact on others.

There is an end goal of souls being saved, but there is a slowing down and stopping for the one.

That was Jesus' method. Because He knew He was going to die at 33, there was no desire for Him to build lifelong workers for His ministry. Not that He would have done that even if He had lived longer. He, instead, wanted disciples who would take the Gospel toward the ends of the earth for their lifetimes. He was intentional with the few years He had with them. Although they were only a handful of years, He did more in that time than the Pharisees could have done in a lifetime.

You may ask, "What could God do with a thirty-second or a sixty-second video?" The truth is that God can do just as much and more with sixty-second videos that are produced from a someone whose heart is sold out to Jesus than He can with sixty years from someone who lives a compromised Christianity.

Kids Receive When We Are Consistent

I learned something in 2020 and 2021 that no stadium, youth rally or conference could have taught me. I learned how to be consistent when all I see is a seed. I learned this in the summer of 2020 as I went to my garage to film videos. I trusted and believed that every video I made would be a chisel in the hand of God on the hardened hearts of this generation. I knew that God would move every time I spoke. I believed that one day the kids who saw the life I was living consistently and heard the words I was sharing would be saved.

I have a different perspective of social media than some. To me, social media is not something that leads us away from our relationship with God. I believe that it is something that gives my relationship with God purpose and worth. I do not keep the salvation that I have received to myself. Social media is a place where every day I give it away. I have received an encounter; therefore, I give an encounter through the Holy Spirit. Social media is only a dark place if believers are not participating in it.

Darkness dwells where Christians do not. For too long, Christians have hidden from darkness. Light should never hide from darkness. Social media is just as vital as a car or a plane that a missionary would take to the church or the nation where he was called to preach. Whatever social media platform you choose to use, it is your digital vehicle to take the greatest news on the planet to those who would never have heard it prior to your coming.

If Not Now, When?

The digital space is an additional method and resource that God has entrusted to His Church. Some of the great men and women of God who had an impact on me in my early twenties were in person, but most I saw through a YouTube video. I would watch sermon after sermon and listen to podcast after podcast that was inspired by the messages of these men and women of God. These messages shaped me as a man, grew my faith and challenged me to live boldly for God in a culture where that was rare.

Can you see it? Can you see your mind begin to question whether you are allowed to do this? Can you see those fears and doubts you have had of evangelizing digitally diminish in comparison to the reward of souls that could be saved?

There is a great invitation happening at this very moment. As I sit here in my living room, God has predestined this moment for you right now. This is the moment for you to enlist into taking the Good News to the digital space.

Take every excuse you have and lay it at the feet of Jesus. Because of the world in which we live and because of technology, it is no longer *if* you can go preach the Gospel, it is *when*.

The rules have changed in this generation. God is entrusting His Church with much more. And believe it or not, the method may have changed, but the mission and spirit did not. When I began to preach in 2009, I showed up in person. Week after week and year after year, I arrived to preach in the same public schools. I made sure that the kids at the schools could be certain of one thing: if I was on their campus, they would be fed pizza and their hearts would be full.

They would leave the gym or auditorium with the message of Jesus. It is the same thing now. Although I still preach in person, I choose to also consistently show up on my phone to share with youth the message that changed my life.

From Discipleship to Conversion

Remember that verse that says some people plant, some people water but Christ makes it grow (see 1 Corinthians 3:6)? This verse gives us hope that God wastes nothing. Discipleship unto conversion is the method of winning souls in Gen Z. It is the method that will create a sustaining, long-lasting relationship with Christ. Discipleship unto conversation is where kids begin a journey of learning the teachings of Jesus, hearing the teachings of Jesus and seeing the teachings of Jesus so that they can realize that He is the greatest thing on this planet and choose to follow Him.

This is much more costly for us as Christians. This type of conversion to Christianity does not happen conveniently in twenty minutes with people we will never see again. This type of conversion is inconvenient. It invades our personal space. It strips away the rights we think we have. It takes away all of the importance and self-titles that we build for ourselves and leaves us vulnerable.

When we preach a public message for thirty minutes, it is much easier to pretend to be somebody we are not. It is not easy when you invite people to do life with you. "Be imitators of me, just as I also am of Christ" (1 Corinthians 11:1) are scary words if you live them sincerely. Suddenly, the greatest teaching does not come from the heroic stories in your sermons, but it comes from the epic failures of your life.

Discipleship unto conversion truly is where God takes the weakness of a man and perfects His power. As He shines His glory through the weakness of men and women, only one name can be praised: the name above all names, Yeshua, Jesus.

I am not throwing away a long-used style of preaching. I am simply inviting us to see evangelism in a different light so that it can better reach this generation. Gen Z longs to follow a person more than they do a platform. They long to see God lived out in our everyday lives. They long to see consistency in a world that is not consistent.

Remember that Gen Z has grown up in the world of information and misinformation, where politicians' lies are painted as truth, morality is subjective, injustice is everywhere and church denominations battle each other on theology. Gen Z is crying for one thing, and it is not who can prove a point and be right in a conversation. It is who can live the Good News and model it in a way that inspires them to do the same. Gen Z discusses death far more frequently and casually than those of us who are older. What is stopping us from talking about the only One in the universe who is worth dying for?

I am pretty sure there were many other teachers in Israel whom the disciples could have followed. What made them follow Jesus? He was different. He was one who walked in authority and power. He was not afraid to live the message He preached. That was why they followed Him.

If You Are Persecuted, Thank God

I have begun recently to learn about how the Church in Iran has flourished under great pressure and persecution, and how great crusades and big ministry events have proven to do little in countries in the East. As I watched a documentary called *Sheep Among Wolves*[1] and had conversations with underground church leaders, I found that many of the methods used to win the lost in the East will work in the West, but not all the methods we use in the West will work in the East. (If the method we use is not effective across the globe, then I would dare to say it is not fully effective anywhere.)

Believers in the Middle East have come to find a way to lead others to Christ in the midst of persecution, prison and even death. It has not been with enticing words, coffee or donuts that were promised at church. In fact, the promise has not been riches or material blessings. From the stories I have heard of people who have lived there, their model is death before disobedience to Christ. For the Iranian Church, the highest joy of a believer and the greatest price of a Christian is simply Christ Himself.

There is going to come a day in which the methods of the East will truly become the methods of the West. Although we are not in full-blown persecution in the West, the tides are changing. More and more, we are seeing believers persecuted and censored for their views and beliefs in the Bible. As persecution rises in the Church and we see our religious liberties slowly stripped away, take heart—it is all part of God's plan. It is purifying the Church and, believe it or not, it has historically been God's method to grow the Church.

The people of Israel, for example, multiplied under the hand of Pharaoh (see Exodus 1:12). And the Church grew rapidly under the Roman Empire, as demonstrated in the book of Acts. If and when your eyes see the days of persecution, take heart. The life that you live for Christ as you invite people to follow Him will bear the greatest fruit.

Now is our moment to disciple youth unto conversion. We should create content, whether it is a post, a video or some other form of media to share Jesus with the world. Do not downplay the souls that can come to Christ just because you are not in a stadium. May the next Jesus movement we see be a Jesus movement of disciples.

YOUR DIGITAL MISSION

Sometimes people think that being led by the Spirit means you are like the wind—spontaneous and unpredictable. But being led by the Spirit does not mean you cannot grow roots and be part of a community. Long-term evangelism and discipleship require the mindset of a Crock-Pot rather than a microwave. Commit to the process to see others come to know Christ. Be led by the Spirit as you establish yourself, build trust and share your life and the Gospel with others.

Pray this with me.

Jesus, I commit to long-term evangelism and discipleship. I commit to no longer settling for a hand raised or a prayer prayed. May I inconvenience myself as I invite people to follow me as I follow Christ. May I love the last, the least and the lost. And may I care for the hearts of the people with whom I speak. Forgive me if I have loved crowds and hated people. Help me love the one as much as I do the ninety-nine, and help me grow roots where You have placed me. In Jesus' name, Amen.

For training resources on this chapter's content, visit brian barcelona.com/dontscroll/.

The Rules Have Changed

I want you to say this with me out loud: the rules have changed.

Say it again: the rules have changed.

One more time, out loud: the rules have changed.

Now more than ever, the Church has a mission field that looks different from all previous ones. The digital mission field is every tribe, every tongue and every nation. This mission field requires everyone working together to reach it. And the potential of what God can do is great.

Ten or twenty years ago, no one could have dreamed that the apps and websites we have used to post pictures of family, to show places we have traveled and to display food we have eaten would become the same vehicle to see souls saved, discipled and sent. We could never have guessed that Instagram, Facebook and TikTok would be ways that the Gospel would go forth.

Obviously, I cannot predict the future, but I can tell you what I believe is coming by looking back in time. And I want to do that by introducing you to a couple of people who have unique roles in what God is doing digitally. They are faithful, anointed and average people who took a leap of faith and believed that God would do a miracle with their simple yes. Just as the boy in John 6 gave up his lunch of fish and bread and saw the multitudes fed, these two have given up their lives and have seen the multitudes fed the Word of God.

In 2021, I had the opportunity of training a few pastors from a church in Dallas called Gateway that is led by Pastor Robert Morris. One of the pastors I trained in TikTok and digital missions was a man in his sixties named Lamar Slay. He had been in ministry for many years, loved God and had a desire to reach and preach to youth.

He expressed that he would have liked to go into schools to preach or hold youth conferences, but he felt that his age limited him a little bit. But his humility and eagerness to sit through a training session gave him a voice to this generation. He could never have guessed what God would do as he stepped into the digital mission space.

Lamar came up to me excitedly after we did our training and said, "Brian, I'm going to launch a TikTok page. I'm going to call it 'The Father Guy,' and I'm going to share with kids the different things a father would."

I thought, *Wow. That's cool.* I was not sure how or if this page would grow, but his willingness and simple yes excited my heart. He started his page that day by sharing prayers and truths from the Bible, and he captured the heart of a father by giving his wisdom and love to the next generation. He shot his videos at his home, many times in front of his chicken coop. I thought it was awesome. There was no hype production or fancy cameras—just a genuine heart and a love for God. And that is the very thing that this generation needs.

Over the next few weeks and months, I got messages about his videos going viral and his page quickly growing to forty thousand followers. But the statement that touched my heart the most came in a text he sent me one day.

"Brian, I want to thank you," the text said. "I don't get invited too often to preach to youth anymore because of my age, and you have made me cool again. You've made me cool with my grandkids because they now follow me. You've given me a voice to youth again."

> **There was no hype production or fancy cameras—just a genuine heart and a love for God.**

Let me tell you again: the rules have changed. Lamar's story demonstrates what I believe God is continuing to do. Evangelism—the proclamation of the Gospel—looks different in every generation. It is our job to know what it looks like in our day and age. You can see that age does not matter, cool clothes do not matter, a bright personality does not matter, fancy cars do not matter nor does a big house matter. What matters is the love of Jesus flowing from your life into that camera onto someone's screen.

Think about the kid who is on the verge of suicide, the kid who has been abused, the kid who is in the middle of his or her parents' divorce, the kid who is strung out on drugs and the kid who feels depressed and alone. They do not care about any of those material things that I just listed. What matters is that God's hand is touching their life through your willingness to obey.

Let me give you a story of someone else who has been faithful to the Lord without caring about the stage or platform. She has mothered her children and stood by her husband. She has lived the Bible quietly and faithfully, prioritizing and allowing God to form *in* her more than what He would ever do *through* her. This person is my wife.

Marcela truly does not like being in the spotlight. For almost seven years, she has stood by my side as the greatest wife and most phenomenal mother. She has championed me in the best of times and the hardest of times. When I pivoted to preaching digitally, although she did not understand it, she supported it. Little did she know that she, too, would be entering the digital mission space shortly after I did.

In September of 2020, God placed a burden on Marcela's heart to equip and empower women. This burden came from a journey that had started in 2019 to see women of God rise up. After gathering together weekly with women in our One Voice community in which they prayed together, read the Word together and grew in relationship together, her desire to see this replicated became evident.

After hearing God speak, and with many confirmations and many dreams, the Lord had my wife's yes. Day after day she would tell me of her desire to equip and empower moms and daughters to help them share their faith and pray. She wanted to see a women's movement raised up in America and the nations—one that would not be fueled by feminism but by faithfulness. She wanted to see a women's movement that would be centered around Jesus and prayer.

A month earlier we had moved from Los Angeles to Dallas, Texas, in obedience to what God had told us. After a month of unpacking and settling in, Marcela and a spiritual daughter of ours, Lauren Bedola, were upstairs discussing what this women's movement would look like and how it would grow. This conversation led to what The Well, which is what my wife's movement is called, would look like as they digitally gathered women to pray.

What if women gathered digitally as the women in the Bible did physically at the well? And what if they prayed instead of just discussing random things? Marcela and Lauren said we should base it on John 4 and Luke 1. They wanted to empower women to have true relationships like Mary and Elizabeth did in Luke 1, and they wanted to take what Jesus did for them and tell everybody like the woman at the well did in John 4. It would not matter what background women came from, as all were welcome to pray and encounter Jesus.

For about thirty minutes they went back and forth with various names for their Instagram account. I even threw in a few of my suggestions that were quickly thrown out. That is when they decided to call it @womenwellgathering. This name was key, because it described the movement (and also there were not many other names available on Instagram).

When they asked me what I thought, I said, "I'm not sure how this name will go, but if that's what God is saying, then do it."

"Let's build an Instagram page, go live and post content for women," Marcela said. As lovingly as I could, I told my wife that I did not think anyone grew anymore from Instagram, but to go for it if she wanted to.

I was very wrong. In one night, @womenwellgathering organically grew to over seven thousand followers. I could not believe it. I thought it was a glitch, and told my wife there was no way it could be real.

But it was real. Women from around the world began to gather every day to pray on Instagram lives, and from October 1, 2020, until now, the live videos are continuing. These women have been equipped and empowered to lead where God has called them. The testimonies are wild, including salvations, healings and women receiving their callings. The Well has been a digital secret weapon God has used to reenlist one of the greatest armies that heaven has: moms, daughters and women of all walks of life.

Evangelism Is Not a Stage in a Park

As I have started traveling again, I have experienced a fantastic confirmation of the digital reach. There have been times when I have been getting ready to preach that someone comes up to me and my team and says, "Hey I've seen your TikTok videos," or "We've seen your content on Instagram."

Can you see it? Can you see what I am talking about? Because of the digital reach of my videos, I start preaching to the audience long before I get to the event. This truly is an hour when the faithful, and not just famous, will have a moment to be as effective as the heroes in the faith before us.

Evangelism is no longer something you do—it is something you live with your day-to-day life on public display. You will live out those words, "Follow my example, as I follow the example of Christ" (1 Corinthians 11:1 NIV). That is evangelism. Our lives are put on public display so that those around us will know Christ.

We are no longer limited to a twenty-minute slot on a stage. Because of the digital mission space, we have an opportunity to take people with us everywhere we go. Day by day, we can share the Gospel as much as we can. Every place, moment or situation in our life now presents an opportunity to share the Good News of Jesus.

Some of the greatest videos I have made have come when I have been in the most random places—the park, a car or even a restaurant. My ability to share the Good News is not hindered by anything. And everyone can take up a calling to evangelize and be a part of all that God is doing right now. Whether you are working a full-time job, are re-tired or are going to school full-time, you can be a digital missionary. Whether you are a high schooler, in junior high or even in elementary school, you can be a digital missionary and join what God is doing.

> **Because of the digital reach of my videos, I start preaching to the audience long before I get to the event.**

What Is God Doing?

Why is God using the digital space in such a profound way? The answer is simple: It is the era in which we are living. While church attendance is declining on a national level and people are falling away from the faith, God's desire to save souls from the pit of hell can now be accomplished by a device that everyone carries. From phones and laptops to iPads and tablets, there is rarely a place where God cannot reach someone digitally.

As times get darker and sin increases, grace abounds even more (see Romans 5:20). Even though things are getting worse in the world around us, reaching the world with the Gospel may seem easier in these next ten years. This is true,

I believe, because lights seem a whole lot brighter in rooms that are dark.

Take courage! As with others who are reading this book, you are part of a great generation and a great harvest. You are part of a time in Church history that will be spoken of many years from now. As we have honored the missionaries who have gone to nations before us, especially those who were the first to go out, this generation is a part of the first wave of true digital evangelism. We do not need expensive equipment or high production to carry the message of God.

Prepare for Censorship

Jesus says that we must carry out the works of Him who sent us as long as it is day (see John 9:4). Night is coming when no man can work. There may be a day in which the Word of God is greatly censored in the West, and the people of God are persecuted. There may be a day in which cancel culture tries to cancel the cross.

If you are unfamiliar with what cancel culture is, you only have to turn on the news. Every day, people who have different views and opinions, primarily ones that are based on the Bible or conservative ideas, are being canceled. What this means is that if you have a different viewpoint, groups of people may rally against you and encourage others to bash you, disown you and hate you. Some companies have even gone to the extent of removing people from being able to use their platforms in the name of unity and being fair. Does this not sound like something that Jesus promised would happen? "And you will be hated by all because of My name"

(Matthew 10:22). There may come a day in which it is so dark that our work must take on yet another method.

Although it is dark in our nation and our world, it is not yet night. Your ability to read this book is proof of that. There is still much work to be done, and there is still much preaching to be done. There are many healings to be done, and there are many prayers to be prayed.

If we are the light of the world (see Matthew 5:14), that means we were created for dark places. Darkness can only continue to dwell in places in which we as Christians do not.

What a shame it would be if all Christian content was taken off platforms. Imagine going to your favorite apps but no longer being able to see Gospel messages because the Bible was deemed hate speech. Imagine only being able to watch biblical content that is filtered by the government. This may sound unrealistic, but when you think about it, we are not far from that. Many countries around the world use these exact filtering methods. There are even some social apps in the United States that have defined hate speech as anything that makes others feel immorally inferior.

Censorship is not a matter of *if* at this point; it is a matter of *when*. If true messages of the Bible are actually censored in the years to come, how fast and how hard would we work to spread the news of Jesus? If we choose not to spread the Gospel digitally now, we will regret that we did too little. We must do all that we can with what we have to see this generation reached.

Be encouraged that difficult and pressing times produce more out of a believer than times of comfort. And with this next decade ahead of us, let's do all that we can to gather data, win souls and disciple people for the Kingdom of God.

How to Evangelize Digitally

Digital evangelism starts with acquiring a heart for those who are lost. Allow yourself to repent for any judgmental thoughts you have had in your heart or mind toward those who do not know Jesus. Then, ask the Lord what He wants to share with people. Believe it or not, some of the most viral videos we have had have been the simplest ones. They have been ones about hearing God's voice, reading simple Bible verses and sharing truths of God's character and nature.

Allow the simplicity of what you share to be the foundation of every post. Remember that you are going to reach believers naturally, but your heart for those who are lost will flow to those who are not saved.

Make posting videos every day a priority as you would prioritize a date with somebody. Be faithful and consistent, as consistency is the currency of this generation. Just as methods change, remember that platforms change. Whatever platform allows you to preach, preach.

As evangelism has evolved, so has discipleship. Remember that Gen Z can connect their emotions to a screen in ways that previous generations could not. Do not write off Zoom, FaceTime or social media livestreams as places that a person cannot encounter God or be discipled. We have seen some of the most powerful moments of baptisms and sermons preached through screens.

Let me give you instructions on how to use these platforms. It is actually quite simple. Once you have moved past feeling as if you cannot do it, it is as simple as downloading an app. In 2021, those would be Instagram, Facebook, TikTok and YouTube, although these apps may change in the years to come.

You get what I am saying. I am not asking you to get on a plane and go somewhere. I am asking you to simply download an app. Create an account and begin to post content about Jesus.

Be consistent. Do not do it for views. Do it because Jesus is worthy. The digital space does not require charisma or great speeches. You will be effective if you are consistent and genuinely share who Jesus is.

Watch our content @thejesusclubs, on YouTube, TikTok or Instagram. See what we do and do the same. Remember that we will overcome by the blood of the Lamb and the word of our testimony. Sharing the truth of Jesus and the Bible is living the word of your testimony. It is powerful and effective. Do not overcomplicate things.

YOUR DIGITAL MISSION

Download one of the social apps needed to preach, and go through our training provided at brianbarcelona.com /dontscroll/. I cannot wait to see what God does with your yes in the digital space.

The Word
of Your Testimony

We gain faith by hearing the Word. We grow in our faith by hearing stories of the Word of God being lived out. Here are some stories of what Jesus did in and through a company of faithful missionaries who said yes to God. May these stories encourage you to see that God is moving powerfully in the digital sphere. Remember, the spirit of religion will acknowledge what God has done and what He will do, but it will never acknowledge what He is doing. So let's break that spirit right now. Let me share some of the wildest stories of what we have seen in the digital space so far.

■ ■ ■

My good friend Shane, a former police officer and Afghanistan veteran (@shane.winnings), left the police force to join us at The Jesus Clubs and preach the Gospel. Shane has reached millions around the world. These are some of the stories of what God has done with and through his life. This is his account of the digital mission movement.

Brain Healed on TikTok

This story comes from when I was brand-new on TikTok. I think it was my second live church. The whole reason I began with TikTok was to go live. Once I got one thousand followers, I could do that. Before this particular TikTok live, I was praying and believed that I had heard the phrase "brain issue." The Lord told me it was for church that night. Fast-forward five hours—I began preaching while there were only about forty people online. I said, "I feel like God wants me to pray for someone who has a brain issue."

I asked if anyone on had that, and one woman said yes. She said she had just been diagnosed with a brain aneurism. There was an extremely high risk of it rupturing, and a daughter aneurism was growing on top of it. For the last month, she said she had lived with a headache 24 hours a day.

"Let's pray right now," I said. I asked everyone to stretch out a hand toward the screen.

After I prayed a simple prayer, she replied in all caps, "MY HEADACHE JUST LEFT, and my head feels fuzzy, like warm."

I was freaking out, and everyone was commenting, "Praise God. This is a miracle." When she went to the doctor about a week later for a brain scan, both aneurisms had completely disappeared.

"This is impossible," the doctors said. "Aneurisms like this don't disappear, not in a week. It might be able to shrink in a year, but we fully expected them to rupture, and yours could have been fatal."

She testified to the doctor that she had been healed over TikTok. She created a video sharing her testimony. When I followed up eight months later, she still had no headaches and was completely healed. The next week, there were two hundred people on the livestream, because people had made videos testifying about seeing her being healed.

Self-Harm Scars Healed

After the message on another live, I was praying for the sick, like I do every time. The Lord said to pray for self-harm scars to disappear. I was praying first for people's minds and hearts to be healed. One girl commented, "That's for me. I have scars on my legs and arms and God touched my heart. I feel like I have hope again."

I felt the Lord say to pray for the scars to disappear, so I had everyone reach a hand toward the screen. She started freaking out in the comments saying that her scars had just gone away. She sent pictures in which the scars were no longer visible. They were completely gone. TikTok banned the video, calling it violent content.

■ ■ ■

Timothy Bruce (@timothy.brucee) is a young man I have had the privilege to see grow in the faith. He has traveled with me around the world and has seen God move powerfully. This is his account of the digital mission movement. In his own words:

Salvation

There was a young person who commented on a video I made about the reality of hell. His comment read, "Haha f your God. I hate Him."

I replied and said, "And still He loves you."

The kid replied and said, "Ok. You have my attention. Tell me why I should turn to God. Give me one reason."

I responded and said, "You hate Him boldly, yet He loved you boldly by dying for you. You reject His love, yet He waits to accept you. You want a reason, but you don't see that He's the only option."

I went to sleep. The next morning, I saw that this kid was trying to contact me by commenting on the video and sending me messages. He told me that he had had a dream in which there was a man in a white robe. When he heard the man's voice, it was different from any other voice he had ever heard. He knew it was Jesus and that he needed to follow Him. So, he gave his life to Jesus, and for about six months has been going through discipleship. I am still connected with him, and he has been asking questions constantly about God.

Freedom from Suicide

I planned a big TikTok live that I promoted, and about halfway through, a specific kid jumped on. He started saying that he was at the end of his rope and that he was going to kill himself. He seemed pretty serious—you can never know, but it is better to take those kinds of words seriously.

I was talking to him when I noticed that he had dropped off. There were about eighty to one hundred kids watching at the time. I told them all to jump off the live, go to his page and encourage him. The number on my live dropped about twenty or thirty people as most of the kids went to encourage him. I finished the message, and at the end of the live, I spoke about inviting the Holy Spirit into our lives so that we can hear His voice.

This specific boy reached out to me at the end and said, "I was on your live and heard the voice of God tonight.

It changed everything." He did not want to end his life anymore.

Discipleship

There was a really influential kid on TikTok who had over a million followers. He followed me after seeing my videos about God. He reached out and said that he really wanted to follow Jesus, so we started talking on a regular basis. His hunger for God started increasing.

One day, he decided to get baptized, so he jumped on our Zoom and got baptized. He then created a separate Christian account and started preaching the Gospel. The new account quickly blew up. He started leading kids to Jesus. When he was with unbelieving friends, he would call me and have me preach the Gospel to them. He still is following God, loves Jesus, is a disciple and is preaching the Gospel.

Healing

At the end of every live, I give time for signs and wonders. The other night on a live, this kid was complaining about having really bad stomach problems. He kept saying it really hurt, so we prayed. After that, in the comments he was freaking out because all his stomach pain had gone away. He was completely healed. There are probably twenty or thirty healings every live.

Another time, a girl got healed of a bad fever. Someone commented, "I'm going on vacation in two days and my sister just got a fever." I just commented the word "praying" to let her know that I would pray for her sister. Not long after that, she commented about her sister. "Wow. God is amazing. She's not a morning person at all, and she's feeling better than ever."

■ ■ ■

Janelle Kightlinger (@janelle.kightlinger) is a faithful leader in One Voice. She is also the director of The Jesus Clubs. She is a former schoolteacher who became a missionary with us and now helps steward missionaries and collaborators across the country with The Jesus Clubs. This is her account of the digital mission movement. In her own words:

Baptism

We baptized an eighteen-year-old girl over Zoom. Before we baptized her, she asked if we could baptize her siblings. She went and got her siblings, and they were all baptized together. The youngest was elementary-age. It was so cool to see. She had connected with us through TikTok, and her siblings got connected through her.

Freedom from Suicide

A student texted into Community, our text-in platform, that he wanted to commit suicide, so a team member shared the hope he had found in Jesus and gathered the team to pray. The next morning, we heard back that he had not taken his life and wanted to know how to follow Jesus.

Discipleship

Someone recently got baptized on Zoom. He had started following us a few months earlier and joined the Zooms just to watch. It is such a picture of discipleship unto conversion.

■ ■ ■

David Latting (@david.latting) is a true man of God in his generation. He is one of the most profound Gen Z voices I have ever known. His life has echoed truth, and his uncompromised belief in God has been responsible for thousands knowing Jesus. These are his accounts of the digital mission movement. In his own words:

Meet Up

The Lord is moving, and He is moving powerfully. There are hundreds of Christian creators online, and by God's will, some of us have been able to meet up. There is one specific meetup that changed my life and many others. About sixty on-fire believers stayed in the same house together and saw the Lord move powerfully.

On one of the nights, four nonbelievers walked in the house, one Muslim and three atheists. By the end of the night, all the nonbelievers were on fire for Jesus. They have now created disciples, and one is even leading a mission movement in Africa to help starving children. We often see American Christians converted by prayer but then persuaded to complacency. These believers, however, are making disciples; they are making a difference.

Do not be discouraged. God is moving, and these testimonies are just the beginning. These testimonies are a glimpse of the hundreds of lives the Lord is changing every day. The Lord is using social media to help gather fiery Christians to stand up against complacency and declare a war on inaction. Generations before us have used radio and television to reach hundreds of millions. In my generation, we are using social media to reach billions.

From Sorrow to Laughter

This second story showed me truly how much the Father cares for me. I was heartbroken, depressed and full of anxiety. I wanted the people online who were feeling the same way I did to feel okay, so I recorded two videos encouraging other broken people. I filmed a video in which I was weeping and pouring my heart out. After I filmed, I just began to weep even more. I could not believe I was telling other people to be okay without being okay myself.

When I went to post my video, I realized that I had accidentally filmed in slow motion. While that might not seem like a big deal, it made my weeping voice sound so weird. Hearing myself speak in slow motion made me laugh out loud! At that moment, the Lord allowed me to experience joy and laughter after not having felt them for months. We serve a good God who is full of humor.

■ ■ ■

Jacob Coyne (@jacob.coyne) has truly been a man of peace, a man of the Word and a man who demonstrates the love of Jesus. His dedication to see suicide end in Gen Z and his heart for the unseen person truly is the fuel behind this powerful digital missionary. This is his account of the digital mission movement. In his own words:

Virtual Stadium Crusades

On July 27, 2021, I opened my Bible to Matthew 28, pressed the "Go Live" button on Instagram, and told my virtual congregation of 87,000 followers that I would be preaching about their calling in the Lord. This was a message that led to a virtual altar call. After twenty minutes of preaching, I provided an opportunity for people to join me virtually to talk and pray. I explained from Mark 16:18 that we are told to "lay hands on the sick, and they will recover." I believed that the sick could be healed during this live stream.

One by one, people joined me in the video chat to receive prayer and healing. The last to join was a teenager. The young man had dislocated his shoulder and said he could not move his arm without excruciating pain, which he described as a 9.5 out of 10.

I said to my new friend, "Wouldn't that be awesome if Jesus healed you right now?"

"Yo! That would be awesome!" he replied.

I continued, "Let's pray right now that the Holy Spirit will touch you, that Jesus' hand will touch that shoulder of yours and that you will be able to move it just as well as your other arm."

I then asked everyone watching to join in prayer for the young man.

I simply prayed for healing in the authority of Jesus' name, commanding the shoulder to realign.

"Every muscle, bone ligament and tendon, be realigned in the name of Jesus Christ. I command all the pain to leave right now."

Live on screen, the young man's shoulder visibly popped back into place. His face filled with surprise and wonder as Jesus healed his shoulder and removed all the pain.

He described what he was feeling as electricity flowing through him. He then felt a click and had full range of motion. The pain was gone! He kept poking his shoulder in amazement at the physical healing that had just taken place.

"I came on this live because my faith was wavering between Islam and Christianity. I had decided that if Jesus healed my arm, I would literally give my life to Jesus," he admitted to me.

I then took the opportunity to lead my new friend in a prayer inviting Jesus into his life. I asked him if he had a Bible and encouraged him to read the book of John. I then messaged him privately to help him continue to grow with Jesus. I simply used the tools I had in my hand to share the

Gospel and pray for people, which led to a miraculous healing and salvation for a young teen.

■ ■ ■

Amy Ayala (@amylynnettee) has been catalytic to seeing youth saved in Los Angeles. Amy has never let her limitations or what she did not have stop her from going after God and seeing the lost saved. Her passion for souls is contagious, and her love for people is truly shown in the stories you are about to read. This is her account of the digital mission movement. In her own words:

Digital Mission Field

One of the craziest experiences I had with TikTok was at the very beginning when my page had just been created. I was encouraged by other creators to go live to see what would happen. I was a little hesitant since I did not know what to expect. I thought that maybe ten people at the most would jump on, but I wanted to give it a shot either way. I remember not knowing what to preach, so I began thinking of the Gospel presentations we had given when The Jesus Clubs were running on high school campuses.

I gave one of my favorite messages, "The Struggle Is Real, but So Is God." That night over two hundred people joined for an unannounced, random live session. What happened that night I would have never believed could happen online. When it came time to invite people to be saved by Jesus Christ, I said, "If you want to accept Jesus as your Lord and Savior today, type in the word *me.*"

In that moment, I was able to count around seventy people who typed in "me." I realized quickly that over one hundred people wanted to accept Jesus into their heart. I began praying for them and said, "If you prayed this prayer, type in the word *saved*."

I watched as all these usernames commented in real time. In that moment, God showed me that behind the usernames were souls who were being brought into the Kingdom. What seemed like a random live to me was a purposeful plan in the heart of God to go after the lost and make them found.

That night God showed me that social media, including TikTok, is a real mission field. Social media is not a form of entertainment or something I could use to pass the time because I was stuck inside due to COVID-19 restrictions. This medium was something I could pour myself into. I was to serve this field and love the sheep.

God continued to do the miraculous. For the next three months, I went live on a nightly basis from 8 to 11 p.m., sometimes going until midnight. God allowed me to witness a digital revival. Hundreds of people from all over the world began joining. There was a hunger for the Word of God as I had never seen before. Lives were being saved, changed and made new by Jesus!

Baptism

God began to deepen my heart for digital missions. What happened next flipped my world upside down. He reminded me that these were real souls. God was reaching people in their homes, cars, rooms and closets. He was reaching them wherever they were and in whatever time zone they were.

During these three months, I began to recognize a lot of the usernames that were joining every night. There was a woman who would always join. She would comment every night on what was being taught, and she would say that her sons watched the live sessions with her. One night, I mentioned that there were going to be baptisms the following week at the church I was attending.

I was not able to attend the Sunday of the baptisms, but another follower sent me a video testimony of the lady who watched with her sons. She showed up to receive baptism for herself and her sons. When the pastor asked her how she found the church, she replied, "TikTok." When I saw the video, tears flooded my eyes.

"Believe in the Lord Jesus, and you will be saved, you and your household" (Acts 16:31). I saw this verse come to life as I watched this woman and her two sons be led by the Spirit and get baptized.

These are real lives and real families that are being filled with a love for Jesus and led to live a life of surrender! These are not meaningless one-minute videos or worthless live sessions. These are eternity-shifting moments where God is reaching His sons and daughters with His love.

■ ■ ■

Kala Maclain Boss (@maclainboss) has been one of our missionaries since 2017. She has served faithfully alongside my wife and me. We have watched her grow from being a quiet assistant to becoming a roaring evangelist. We believe her journey has just begun, and there will be great miracles that she will witness throughout the rest of her life. This is her account of the digital mission movement. In her own words:

Healing

One of my favorite testimonies that I have seen since sharing the Gospel on digital platforms was one that can only be attributed to the power of God—it was not my powerful words or prayers. We were on a tour called *Gen Z for Jesus* in October of 2020. Each night we were in a different city. As we would worship, share the Gospel and pray for healing in person, we would also go live on our accounts for those who were not able to attend. We wanted them to be able to encounter Jesus as well.

On the second or third night of the tour, we were on a high school field in Louisiana. Toward the end of the event, a couple of people had words of knowledge about a few different things that the Lord wanted to heal. I do not remember what they were, but I remember putting a comment up on the TikTok live I was doing. I asked if anyone watching was dealing with what they had said in the words of knowledge. Several people said yes and shared what they needed healing for.

Not wanting to turn the screen on myself, I put something super simple in the comments—"praying for you."

I continued to walk around so that those on the live could see those who was being prayed for in person and what God was doing. As we began to ask in person if anyone was experiencing healing, I also typed a comment asking if anyone on the live was healed. It was crazy. There were six or seven people who began sharing that they had been totally healed!

God healed them through a phone screen. We did not even pray for them over the microphone, and I did not pray for them out loud. They experienced the healing and the power of God virtually through a livestream of an event just as the people who were attending in person were experiencing healing.

Hunger for Jesus

Another testimony that I have seen in the digital space involves my own story of stepping into posting content on social platforms. I have never really enjoyed or been attracted to social media, and I never imagined that I would be one to share the Gospel digitally. When I was asked to start posting content to reach a generation digitally, I was not super excited about it. But I knew I had to say yes.

I had no idea what to do, and I was very nervous. If this was the direction in which the Lord was leading, however, I was willing. I had been told of the hunger that this generation had for truth on platforms such as TikTok, but in all honesty, I did not believe it until I saw it. I had been told that lives would be impacted and transformed as I shared who Jesus is and the truth of His Word, but I had no idea that I could be used by God in a significant way in the digital space. I had seen it work for people on our team, but I wrote their success off as them being anointed preachers.

Little did I know what God could do with my simple yes. Within the first couple days of posting, I was blown away as people posted comment after comment. They were responding to videos that I posted about Jesus, about hearing God and about the simple Gospel. I received many messages from those who were hungry and desperate to know God, who had been healed through a prayer, who had encountered the presence of God through a video or a live or who wanted to follow Jesus but did not know how.

There is a generation that is desperate for truth, and if we do not show up and point them to the truth, someone else will point them to a lie.

■ ■ ■

Social Media Salvations

I hope your heart has been filled with faith as you have read these stories. You may be wondering if this is real. Is this truly authentic? Can God really touch someone's life through a screen? Can a healing really take place through a screen? Can addictions truly be broken through a video? Are those conversions with Christ authentic?

You would not be the first one to be skeptical of Jesus' work. Similar people existed in the Bible, too. We can take one of two positions when hearing a testimony. The first position we can take is to stand on the sideline and criticize what we think should have happened. Position number two is to celebrate that the Kingdom of God was advanced, and Jesus was made known.

Someone reached out to me once on Instagram after I posted a Zoom baptism we did. Zoom baptisms are something we did throughout the COVID-19 pandemic. We recognized that kids wanted to be baptized, but they were unable to get to a place where they could be baptized. Once a month, kids would sign up to be baptized over Zoom. We would ask them if they believed in Jesus, if He was their Lord and Savior, if they believed He had died on the cross and rose again, and if they were going to follow Him. After we were sure they knew what they were saying yes to, we would baptize them. At 8:00 p.m. Central Time, our team, along with 100 to 250 kids, would jump on Zoom. One by one, the kids would fill up their bathtubs (with appropriate clothing, of course) and dunk themselves. As they did, we would baptize them.

There were even some instances where kids did not have the means to fill up their bathtub—either they did not have a bathtub or they did not have something to plug it to fill it up fully—so they would dump buckets of water on their head in faith and obedience to the Word of God.

Sadly, messages I received said these baptisms were not valid. Some said that because we were not with the kids in person, the baptism was not real. One specific commenter said, "That's not a real baptism, because their whole body was not fully submerged." I read this comment with sadness in my heart. I thought about how easy it is to be caught up in what we think God deems appropriate. Because of this individual's opinions, he missed the work of God that was being done.

I replied, "Is your faith in the amount of water or in the action of obedience to God this young person took?"

Not everything Jesus did was up to par with tradition. I do not think it was common for rabbis to let sinful women wash their feet. I do not think it was common for rabbis to spit in dirt, make clay and rub it in a blind man's eyes for his healing. I do not think it was common for rabbis to tell their followers to symbolically drink their blood and eat their flesh (see John 6:56).

Do you get the picture I am painting? God will never fit into your box. Jesus says, "Blessed is he who is not offended because of Me" (Matthew 11:6 NKJV). What keeps the miracle from coming to us is the offense that we take with the way that Jesus moves.

Results

The greatest results we see have not been numbers, views or comments. The greatest results have been lives that have been changed. You could judge the method, but that will not change what God has done in someone's life. Remember the blind man in John 9? The Pharisees questioned who had healed him. They questioned his family multiple times, and they tried to get the healed man to say that the One who healed him was a sinner. The man's response was, "Whether He is a sinner, I do not know; one thing I do know, that though I was blind, now I see" (verse 25).

The countless souls who have come to know Christ through the simple videos we have made could not care less about the method or the way that God encountered them. All they know is that they had an encounter with God. God does not need much to speak. According to the Bible, He can talk through a burning bush (see Exodus 3:2–5), through a still, small voice (see 1 Kings 19:12) and even through a donkey (see Numbers 22:28–30).

"I tell you, if [His disciples] stop speaking, the stones will cry out!" (Luke 19:40). Digital missions are not a method of how; they are passion to do whatever it takes to see Jesus made known.

YOUR DIGITAL MISSION

Write down right now what you are believing God to do in your life through digital missions. What stories from this chapter provoked you? Take that note, hold it in your hands as a promise and ask God to move through you. Expectation will always create a space for Jesus to move. Go and make memories with God and let Him speak through you.

Pray this with me:

Jesus, I ask that You would write stories through my life. Give me faith for my unbelief. Heal the sick, save

souls and break the power of darkness through my life.
In Jesus' name, Amen.

For training resources on this chapter's content, visit brian
barcelona.com/dontscroll/.

Character
to Carry the Call

Character **is a word** we use often in the Church, but I think it is misused when we use it to describe an unrealistic standard that we expect from believers. We often use *character* to describe the perfect Christian who does everything right and makes no mistakes. The Christian who does not fail or sin is said to have good character. But I have never seen that definition used to describe the good character of a man or a woman of God in the Bible.

I want to encourage you that even the greatest leaders, both from the Bible and those alive today, have made mistakes. May this give you great hope as you venture to be a digital missionary. Your character is what will sustain you as a Christian and as a digital missionary, especially in the days in which we are living.

Proverbs 24:16 says that the righteous fall seven times and yet rise again. Character is not about the fall; it is about standing back up. This Bible verse points out two things that many of us do not realize. First, righteous people make mistakes. Second, it is not *if* you are going to fall, but *when* you will fall. As believers, we all fall short of the glory of God (see Romans 3:23). But having the character to get back up is the difference between the seventh time and the eighth time.

> **Character is not about the fall; it is about standing back up.**

Character is not perfection. It is the courage to say you are sorry. A coward can make a mistake, blame himself or others, leave God and be bitter. But courageous men and women humble themselves, fully depend on the Lord and know that it is by His grace and mercy that they have anything.

You cannot control the things you will go through in life. You cannot control the words you will hear, the betrayals you will endure, the disappointments you will feel or the many things that will come from the outside to attack you. But you do not have to let those things get to your heart. This is where true character resides. True character is what will keep you in a place of being able to see God move greatly.

Now more than ever before, this could not be truer. Godly character is what is needed, especially in the digital space. Most people judge your appearance, your followers and how good your content is, but God judges who you are when you turn off that screen.

Let me start with the greatest man who ever walked the earth—Jesus. He was a Jew who was born in a heavily religious time who knew who He was at a young age. He knew that one day His identity would cause Him to hang on a cross. I think about the triumphal entry, the palm trees being laid down at His feet and the miracles, signs and wonders He performed for many. As He was doing those things, He knew that some of the people He healed and some who wept tears and gave God thanks would probably be some of the ones who would stand as His jury with Pontius Pilate yelling, "Crucify Him" (see Luke 23:21).

We live in a society that tells us to get rid of people who could be threats. That was never Jesus' model. He allowed those who were weak and broken to travel with Him. He even let a man travel with Him who would steal from Him (see John 12:6) and later betray Him with a kiss to His cheek (see Mark 14:44).

Character goes beyond behavior modification. Character allows you to fulfill the will of God regardless of what is said or done to you. Trust me, as you venture out to preach, there will be many things said and done to you. Your heart must remain firm yet tender, never losing the love that you once had when you started your walk with Christ.

In my view, Jesus' character was most greatly displayed when He stood before Pontius Pilate. While it was truly displayed in the Garden of Gethsemane and on the cross, we also see it in His answers to Pilate regarding His identity. "'You are the King of the Jews?' And Jesus said to him, 'It is as you say'" (Matthew 27:11). His identity was rock solid. He was not fazed at the flogging He had just endured or the betrayal of His close friend Judas.

Think about this. Despite betrayal, beatings and insults, Jesus' identity was not shaken. That is character. Accusations continued to pour in from the chief priests, elders and religious leaders, but the character of Jesus shone through. It was so evident that Pilate asked Jesus, "Do You not hear how many things they are testifying against You?" (verse 13).

Jesus' unshaken character shocked Pilate and moved his heart so much that he had an idea: *I will let the Jews chose between Jesus and Barabbas, a man I know is worse than Jesus.* It is possible that Pilate hoped the crowd would see that Jesus was not as bad as this notorious prisoner.

Pilate asked who the Jews wanted him to release, probably certain that they would say Jesus. Clearly, Jesus' crimes were not as bad. To his shock, the crowd told him to release Barabbas.

Not knowing what he would do with Jesus, he asked, "What shall I do with this man?"

"Crucify Him!" the crowds cried (verse 22).

You have seen this in most Easter plays and Christian movies. But did you ever notice that this was one of Jesus' greatest displays of character? Instead of hurling insults back at the crowd or looking at the people He had once healed and asking, "How could you?" He accepted willfully a death penalty for a crime He had not committed. Not seeking to justify Himself, He gladly changed places with a notorious prisoner who deserved crucifixion.

Unwavering, Christlike character is the only way we are going to survive what is coming to the Church. It is the only way we are not going to fall into the bitterness that has taken so many other believers. We must have character that is rooted in the humility of Christ and that is loyal to the calling of Christ more than the criticism of man. For too long we have let opinions of people, especially people with whom we have no relationship, shape what we do for God. This has to stop. Naysayers and opinions, especially from those who do not know us, can no longer be the walls that cage us in. We have to be secure in Christ and Christ alone.

Naysayers and opinions, especially from those who do not know us, can no longer be the walls that cage us in.

When this is challenging, remember Jesus as He was standing in front of Pilate. Ask God to give you that same understanding of your identity.

Embrace Persecution

You do not have to worry about persecution and hatred, because Jesus promised that it will come. In fact, Jesus warns you not of persecution, but when all men speak well of you (see Luke 6:26). God is more concerned about you falling prey to flattery than He is about you being persecuted. Jesus promises His disciples that we will be hated (see John 15:18–19). It does not say that we might be hated. It says that we will for His sake. In a wonderful turn of events, however, being hated with Christ brings about a greater reward than just being blessed by Christ.

God can deliver you from the need to be accepted and the fear of rejection. True rejection cannot actually happen from any human being, because no human can ever give you true acceptance. The only rejection that you should fear is that which comes from the One who can destroy both your body and your soul (see Matthew 10:26–28). When you catch this revelation, your insecurity, doubts and fears must vanish, just as they had to vanish for Jesus.

Cancel Culture Is Irrelevant Next to Eternity

In a society in which both the Church and the world have an opinion about everything you do, cancel culture can be used as a gift from God. We can look at society's cancel culture as a curse, but I see it as a promise.

The Lord *does* want to cancel all the hope you have placed in yourself, in your platform, in your ministry and in your following. So what if that which you have built is canceled? Human beings cannot cancel the One who formed the foundations of the earth. They cannot cancel the One who formed you in your mother's womb or the One who ripped you from death, hell and the grave. They cannot cancel the worship that takes place day and night, night and day around the throne of God (see Revelation 4:8).

No entity in the universe can cancel the Man who will rip open the skies and be seen by every eye as every knee bows and every tongue confesses that Jesus Christ is Lord (see Philippians 2:10–11). Cancel culture is barely a drop in the ocean of eternity. We must never allow cancel culture to cancel our salvation, nor must we allow that culture to live within the Body of Christ.

I have frequently seen people who are close to me be affected deeply by the comments that are left about things they have said. I have even seen people step away from the digital platform because of criticism and hate. This is why the character on the inside of us must be strong. It must be stronger than the hate we are going to encounter.

Cancel culture must be uprooted from all of us. Remember that cancel culture was created as a weapon to make you bow to ideologies and ideas with which you do not agree.

Good men and women, both religious and nonreligious, have been bullied by this so-called inclusive and loving culture—a culture that says you can belong until you do something others disagree with.

As surely as it is a gift to help us die to ourselves and pick up our cross, it can be a curse if we buy into this belief system. If we begin to cut people out for their mistakes, we must be reminded of a sober biblical promise: "If you do not forgive other people, then your Father will not forgive your offenses" (Matthew 6:15).

When lived out by a believer, cancel culture disempowers the grace God wants to express through us. We can quickly forget the Gospel that was preached to us, as Paul told the Galatians in his day. Paul said, "I am shocked that you are turning away so soon from God. . . . You are following a different way that pretends to be the Good News but is not the Good News at all" (Galatians 1:6–7 NLT).

The world is trying to tell us what the Gospel is, but we must stand true. The Kingdom that Jesus brought is full of forgiveness, grace, surrender, allegiance to God and inward holiness. Remember we are in the world, but we are not of it.

Every generation battles its own version of cancel culture. In the day of Jesus, the bloody Roman colosseums tried to silence the Christians. Today, it is the major tech companies that are trying to silence us. We do not see lions eating believers, but we see accounts being blocked. The method is different, but the spirit is the same.

The incredible thing to notice is that no matter what time or era you live in, from the days of Pharaoh to the 21st century, persecution spreads the Gospel. I say with much hope and joy that as we invade this culture with the love and forgiveness of Jesus, we are about to see one of the most glorious revivals.

Believe the Best in One Another

There have likely been many moments when you have been offended with believers, the Church or the Body of Christ. That is normal. If you grew up in a family, you know that the people we love the most are some of the people who wound us the most.

I am not justifying pain or saying that all situations were right, but I have noticed a few things as a father of three. I have noticed the division that sometimes comes between my daughters—the comparison, the envy and the offense. My greatest desire for my kids in the natural realm is that they would love one another.

I have had many sit-downs with my daughters, Zoe and Everlyse, during which I explain to them that sometimes things are not fair. The Bible never promised us that situations would be fair during our time on earth. It only promises that we would receive reward or loss at the end of our lives based on how we handled situations that we were given.

If there are wounds or offenses that you have carried for many years, you should consider the life of Jesus. He had the right to be the most offended person on the planet. Yet as He hung on the cross, His words were far from revengeful. In fact, they were quite the opposite. He said, "Father, forgive them; for they do not know what they are doing" (Luke 23:34).

These words are powerful. They do not say that what the others did was right, but they open up the space for forgiveness. You are giving the other person the benefit of the doubt that they did not mean to hurt you.

Before you jump to conclusions when you are wronged, remember that Jesus forgave, because those who crucified Him did not see the value of who He was. Regardless of the church that hurt you, the relationship that broke or the family member you have not spoken with for many years, you have an opportunity to live the Gospel.

Hell is not terrified when you blast your offenses on social media to expose the hearts of other people. Hell is afraid when you forgive. Jesus walked in the most religious, hostile culture, and yet He never let the religious, hostile culture walk in Him. This is true character. Following in Jesus' footsteps is what will continue to sustain you as you preach the Good News.

Hell is afraid when you forgive.

Is this not what Jesus did with you? He knows your mess, the filth of your sin, the sin you are ashamed of. When you considered Him an enemy, He still looked at you and said that He wanted you. That is character. I urge you to be quick to forgive, for an offended heart is fertile soil for deception and a seared conscience.

Pause for a moment and ask the Lord to forgive you. Ask others to forgive you, and forgive those with whom you have an offense. Remember the times you have needed forgiveness and mercy. It is now time to give that to others.

All Your Words Are Recorded

Every word you speak in this season is a seed of the fruit you will bear in the next season. Do not speak of someone in a way that his or her Creator would not. Remember that you cannot judge people at the beginning or middle of their lives. You can only judge them at the end of their lives. It is not how you start; it is how you finish.

I believe that this is what is coming to the Church. Forgiveness is what is going to break the back of offense and allow the character of Christ to rest in our lives. To the question of how many times we should forgive, Jesus responded seventy times seven (see Matthew 18:22). If you do not know that math, let me break it down for you. Seventy times seven equals a lot. Forgive a lot. Love a lot. After all, that is what God does with you.

In a world that captures every word you say, be wise as serpents and innocent as doves (see Matthew 10:16). Speak life in a culture of death, and speak wisdom in a culture of stupidity. Jesus knew how powerful His words were, and He refused to fall into the trap of the questions He received from the religious leaders. He simply responded using their own logic so that they realized how foolish their logic was.

As you create content, do not fall into the trap of sharing your anger or frustration about what is taking place in the world. Instead, give the hope of Jesus. Allow God to take your pain and turn it into prophecy. Allow God to take the weak areas of your character and shine His glory through it. Although David had many mess ups in the Bible, we remember him the most by the slingshot that he swung and the stone that hit that giant's head. We admire David's life, because he never quit running toward God.

That is character. Do not quit. And if there are moments in which you fail, get back up. This generation needs your voice.

YOUR DIGITAL MISSION

The best way to sustain your character is to stay submitted to God and to those He places over you. Being a part of a community where others can speak into your life will help you stay on course. Also, reach out to a few trusted leaders to provide you feedback and opportunities for growth. Do not pick and choose what truths in the Bible you will believe. Believe everything that is in the Word of God. Remember that those who remain teachable will always be reachable.

For training resources on this chapter's content, visit brian barcelona.com/dontscroll/.

Decentralized and Unified

The word *decentralization* means to "transfer (control of an activity or organization) to several local offices or authorities rather than one single one."[1] This perfectly fits the description of what God is doing with the digital space, The Jesus Clubs and digital missionaries. The method that many Western churches and organizations use has been built around a central ministry or a central person. We have created hierarchies in which one man hears from God and delivers the Word of the Lord to everyone else.

I am not saying that there are not moments where that is needed or where direction needs to be given from a leader, but for a sustainable, global mission movement, decentralization that is gathered around common values and biblical faith is what is needed. This method will proceed the next great move of God on the earth.

This is the model we see in the Bible. Jesus empowers His followers to depend on what He taught them more than on His physical presence with them. Throughout their journey with Him, He prepared them for His leaving. He told them that He would not always be with them (see Matthew 26:11). Jesus was building a decentralized Church centered around the head, Christ, with the Holy Spirit distributed equally to every believer.

The Bible is the book to which we submit our lives, and it is the book that culture, our past and our economic status come under.

And this could not be truer for the day and age in which we are living. The Holy Spirit is a great equalizer. He empowers the man or woman of God who has been saved for forty years with the same power as He does an eighteen-year-old who just accepted Christ. The Bible is to be the thing that brings believers together. The Bible is the book to which we submit our lives, and it is the book that culture, our past and our economic status come under. Together we work as one, yet we are decentralized. Let me explain what I mean.

From Thousands to Millions

I was on a phone call with a pastor whom I was inviting to be part of The Jesus Clubs. I explained that The Jesus Clubs is a culture, not necessarily a ministry. The Jesus Clubs is known not for its leader or its preachers but for its message and its values.

People who have @thejesusclubs in their bios on TikTok or Instagram are known as truth preachers because they

preach the Bible. They are known for still believing in re-
pentance, holiness, righteousness, the blood of Jesus, the
crucifixion and the resurrection. They are known for still
believing that God heals, God moves and God speaks today
through His Word and the Holy Spirit.

The Jesus Clubs members are known for not bending to the
cultural narrative. We are known for loving truth more than
popularity and for loving the foundation of our faith, knowing fully that Progressive Christianity is not Christianity at all.
We are not perfect—we all make mistakes. There are moments
where I am sure we have all had to watch our own videos to
encourage ourselves. But our hope is in Christ, not in ourselves, and we know that with Him all things are possible.

Are you starting to see how when you have a decentralized
vision you rally behind the things that truly matter in the
Word? We rally around things that bring unity to the Body
of Christ. We are no longer centered around our style. A
charismatic can value a Baptist, because he or she sees the
different roles each part of the Body plays. I believe that the
heart of God is that His Church would be unified. Together,
our mission is the Great Commission.

After sharing this with the pastor, he replied by giving
me the greatest compliment I had received in thirteen years.

"So, who started The Jesus Clubs? Who is the leader?"
he asked. I smiled over my Zoom call but did not answer
his question.

"That is exactly what we have strived for," I said. "The
Jesus Clubs, this digital expression of a Jesus movement,
was never meant to be known by its leader. For too long
ministries have pointed their followers back to the minister
instead of straight to Jesus."

This is a dangerous philosophy of ministry to have, because our lives carry a natural shelf life—death. Our days are numbered, and Jesus' model of discipleship is that those we disciple would be greater and do greater things. "Truly, truly I say to you, the one who believes in Me, the works that I do, he will do also; and greater works than these he will do; because I am going to the Father" (John 14:12). Have you ever thought of that? The ultimate disciple maker built His method and model on encouraging others to do greater things than He had done.

Gen Z will be like John the Baptist who proclaimed His Second Coming. The decentralization of this Jesus movement is what has led thousands to Christ already and what is going to lead millions to Christ in the years to come. And it will be unstoppable.

I believe a billion-soul harvest will start in Generation Z. Who would have guessed that Jesus would make a triumphant entry to this generation not on a donkey, but through a phone? He will come riding on the words of humble believers who faithfully share the Gospel every day through their social media platforms.

The Common Ground of Jesus

From the beginning of this digital mission idea, there has been one thing on our hearts. How can we work together? How can we let our differences be bridges instead of walls? How can mission movements and churches, youth pastors and senior pastors, children's pastors, moms and dads, grandparents, teenagers, young adults and middle schoolers all be brought together?

We discovered that the common ground we would stand on would be that our voices would be used to share the Good News of Jesus. You may be able to shut one of us down, maybe even a handful of us, but shutting all of us down when there are millions of us proclaiming and preaching the name of Jesus is impossible. Our unity is our weapon. Our message of Jesus is our ammunition. We must remember that the more the people of God are oppressed, the more we multiply.

Our unity is our weapon. Our message of Jesus is our ammunition.

The digital mission space does not require a college or seminary degree. Formal schooling is needed and important when you are pursing being a teacher of the Word, but everyone is called and equipped to share the Good News of Jesus. The education level of the disciples was not one of Jesus' criteria when He chose them. In fact, head knowledge would have likely prevented them from following Jesus. Especially when He would say things like telling His disciples to eat His flesh and drink His blood (see John 6:52–58).

Jesus had a decentralized model that empowered people who knew less than He did, who did not have it all together and who did not carry big titles. His only qualifying factor was their willingness to obey in the midst of hardships. The instant obedience of Matthew, Mark, John and the others gave them a seat at the table to make and write history.

Likewise, brothers Peter and Andrew abandoned all they had known to follow this Jewish rabbi. That, too, got them a seat at the table of writing history. Today, God has not changed His requirement of using your life. All He desires is your obedience.

On a Zoom call in July of 2020, I shared with a handful of people an idea I had. I called it a holy experiment.

"What if we would all jump on socials together and preach the Gospel? What if the common theme would be Jesus? What if our audience would always be the next generation? What if we wouldn't compromise the Gospel? What if we talked about real life experiences that we've had with God, such as the baptism of the Holy Spirit, praying for the sick, preaching the Gospel and hearing God? What if we didn't rally around a personality but the person Jesus? What if everyone had the same opportunity to share the Good News of Jesus? What if this digital mission movement wasn't about the famous, but the faithful? What if everyone was invited?"

This is what we did July of 2020.

Not everyone bought in when I shared the idea. Some left that Zoom call and never reached out to us again. Some joined with great hesitancy. Even some individuals on my team did not know how the digital space would fit into their lives.

That is the beauty of this mission, though. This move of God is never meant to fit into our lives. We are meant to fit into what God is doing. This truly was a John 1:37 moment: "And the two disciples heard him speak, and they followed Jesus." That moment was significant because up until this time, John the Baptist's disciples followed him. But the moment John acknowledged that the Lamb of God had come, John's disciples quickly abandoned him to follow the One who had eternal life.

And that is what we did. With our weak, simple yes, a handful of us said, "If Jesus is going this way, then we want to go where He's at. We want to be where He's at. We want

to do what He's doing." That is how The Jesus Clubs movement on TikTok began.

Every day we uploaded post after post. We grew a following quickly, not just as a movement but as individuals. People
from all over the country started posting their own content
about Jesus with their unique voices and styles. We began
to celebrate each other as we watched God honor what we
were doing. Friends I had watched serve God faithfully for
years now had a voice to the next generation.

I can still remember the group messages. Those who had
joined us would text in things like, "My following just grew
to 10k."

"My video just got 30k views."

"This person got healed."

"This person got saved."

The celebration that took place fueled the unity of our
team.

Unity is a key ingredient to decentralization. Ambition, insecurity and control are the death of decentralization, because
decentralization tests the motive of an individual's heart.

We read quite a bit about Matthew, Mark, John and Peter,
but do you ever think about the other disciples you do not
hear too much about? You do not read a lot about what they
did. For whatever reason, Jesus did not choose to give them
a book to write in the Bible. If this is affecting your heart, I
encourage you to ask God why. Do you deem the disciples
who did not get to write part of the Bible less than other
disciples? Or do you think they did not play as significant
of a role in the life of Jesus?

Make no mistake—just because you do not hear of their
great exploits does not mean that demons did not shriek

when they walked by. It does not mean that they did not cast out demons and heal the sick. When we arrive in heaven, we will be greatly surprised at how much certain individuals did for God in their hiddenness, and how little we did for God when we decided to prioritize personal motivations.

If you feel left out or forgotten, or if you have a selfish ambition to be known, may God deliver you now. In the Kingdom of God, everything is opposite. He who humbles himself is exalted. He who exalts himself is humbled. Humility and willingness to be unknown are key ingredients for decentralization.

Unity is critical in a space that is filled with vanity and division.

Unity is critical in a space that is filled with vanity and division. These keys will allow you to be a part of a decentralized movement. They will help sustain what God is doing through your life so that you do not fall prey to the traps that are entangling Christians today.

A Great Harvest Is Coming

If you are wondering how all of this is possible, the answer is that you have to take a risk. When I share this idea with various churches, I am met with the same concerns from leaders, pastors and churches: the ministry will split up because someone besides the main pastor will become too known, people will build brands other than what the church is building, or there could be disunity and a church split.

Can you hear the fear in the responses to what I am sharing? Remember that perfect love casts out all fear, and perfect love for God and one another through Christ Jesus will allow us to flourish.

Over the months that we have done various trainings, I have personally trained hundreds to preach digitally. I have given them everything that I have learned through blood, sweat, tears, prayer and fasting so that they would be able to flourish. We have had the incredible opportunity to train CfAN, a ministry that is responsible for over seventy million souls coming to Christ in Africa, in their use of digital space. Once led by belated evangelist Reinhard Bonnke, this ministry has seen signs and wonders and miracles for decades. It is now led by evangelist Daniel Kolenda.

As evangelist Kolenda and I ate dinner before we trained 150 of their bootcamp students in Orlando, Florida (who are their upcoming evangelists that will go to the nations), I was amazed by a statement that he made.

As I was sharing with him what we were going to be training his people, he said, "Do you know who would have used TikTok, Brian?"

I replied, "Who?"

He said, "Reinhard Bonnke. He was a firm believer in utilizing whatever tool was needed to preach the Gospel." My heart was so encouraged knowing that one of the greatest evangelists who ever lived would not have wasted the opportunity to preach using a digital platform.

We trained their team for three hours, walking them through the why, what and how of digital missions. We knocked down the barriers, the fears and the excuses of the older generation, and at the end of the night nearly every person made his or her first video.

What encouraged me even more was that as this training in CfAN's studios was coming to a close, I said, "Are there any volunteers who would like to make their first video in front of everybody?"

The first person who raised his hand was a dad in his late forties who had been a participant in our training school. I remember this guy because earlier in the training he had told me that his son had told him, "Dad, whatever you do, don't start a TikTok." He got up in front of everybody and presented the Gospel powerfully on his phone. As he hit the post button to share with everyone in the world, the room erupted in celebration.

I asked again, "Is there anyone else who would like to volunteer?" And in the back left corner, a young man with autism quickly shot his hand up.

He said, "I would like to go." He came up, and in front of this room, he made his first Gospel video. I am not going to lie. As he was creating it, I felt tears begin to fill my eyes. After he filmed it and he hit post, again the room erupted with celebration that the Kingdom of God was being advanced.

Why do I share this story? Because sitting in that room were some of the great evangelists of our day, including evangelist Daniel Kolenda and evangelist Nathan Morris from Shake the Nations. Those two alone have led millions to Christ. But on that day, it was the fifty-year-old father and the young man with autism who pioneered the first digital expression of preaching the Gospel for CfAN. And because of great leaders like evangelist Kolenda, they, too, had the ability to share the Good News and write history for God.

There have been many other churches and pastors we have trained who now have hundreds of thousands of followers sharing about Jesus. My heart is truly full of joy because they now have been commissioned beyond their four walls to take the Good News to the ends of the earth. Be encouraged that this way of thinking did not happen overnight for me. And as you have read, the process started with God greatly humbling me in 2020 when I realized the youth of America and the nations could not be reached solely by me or our ministry. But together as one Body, we can see the greatest harvest of our time.

12 Tips for Effective Digital Missions

Read these final words slowly. May the Holy Spirit deposit them into your heart.

1. Use your words wisely, because they are powerful.
   The tongue has the power to bring life or death. That power extends to the words your fingers type on a screen. Our words truly matter. The honor that we sow in this season will be the fruit that we eat in the next.
2. Be mindful of pride. Let the peace of God that surpasses understanding guard your heart. Never believe your own hype. Never live on the praise of people's comments, or you will be crucified by their criticism.
3. Do not fear cancel culture. Acknowledge and praise God in the midst of everything. If we deny Him on the earth, He will deny us before His Father in heaven. Know that you will be hated, despised, mocked and put down, so expect that. You are not greater than Jesus, and that is what happened to Him.
4. Preach the whole Gospel. Keep the main thing the main thing. But in everything you preach, let it come from a place of love.

5. Never allow your heart to grow envious of what God is doing in someone else's life. Celebrate what God does in other people's lives, and the Father will always be gracious to give you more.

6. Celebrate steadfast faithfulness rather than rapid growth.

7. Give yourself grace. As God is patient with you, be patient with yourself. When insecurity and fear knock at your door, allow Jesus to open it and walk you into His stable love.

8. Never put your worth in what God does through your hands. Your worth comes from the One who knit you in your mother's womb, not the things you do for Him. If you are a Gen Zer, this is especially for you. Gen Z, you have been entrusted with an influence and platform that no other generation has ever known. You will be greatly tested. Keep fathers and mothers around you in the faith—those who can tell you no when you are off and who can correct you when you need it.

9. Trust the gray-haired wisdom of fathers and mothers. The Bible says those who do not heed correction are stupid. Know that nothing is new under the sun. God moving uniquely in your generation does not overshadow or negate what He has done in past generations.

10. Know that every generation is given a method to use to bring the Gospel. If that method changes in ten years, move with the Holy Spirit. Do not marry your method. Marry the mission God has given you, which is the Great Commission.

11. Fight for one another. Pray for one another. Community is what will keep us strong.

12. Read your Bible daily, but do not read it just so that you can create content. Let His Word be the ultimate authority in your life, regardless of what culture, politics or religious leaders say. The Bible should always have the last word. Many false truths will arise in the decades to come. Run from those who claim they have some special arrangement with God. Make reading the gospels (Matthew, Mark, Luke and John) a part of every day. Find one thing that Jesus said or did that you can put into practice today.

I look forward one day to meeting in heaven the millions of people who were impacted by those who chose to be digital missionaries. My prayer is that the heart of decentralization would become the norm in the global Church.

YOUR DIGITAL MISSION

Read the previous section above one more time. Which one of the twelve tips is God highlighting to you right now?

Heavenly Father, I receive Your commission to do my part in reaching this generation for Christ. In Jesus' name, Amen.

For training resources on this chapter's content, visit brian barcelona.com/dontscroll/.

Afterword

What we experienced as normal is gone. It will never come back. There is not a magic solution that will return the world to what it knew before 2020. We can only move forward now. I am excited for what God has, and I am eager to see what He is going to do. May your heart be full of faith that when you are in front of someone at a store or when you are on your phone, you can and will preach the Gospel.

To Fathers

There is a great plan that God has for you in this generation. Your age and past failures have not disqualified you. You are needed greatly. This is truly a Malachi moment. "He will turn the hearts of the fathers back to their children and the hearts of the children to their fathers" (Malachi 4:6). I beg you to allow your heart to turn to this generation. As culture—sexual immorality, gender confusion and political agendas—wages war on the children of your nation, will you take a stand?

Will you get up from the shackles of shame and fight for this generation? Will you pray more than you have ever prayed? Will you fast more than you have ever fasted? Will you allow all that God has spoken and done in your life to be spread digitally to kids all over the world?

What I believe shaped Jesus was the influence of His earthly father, Joseph. I am pretty sure Joseph had moments of feeling disconnected from Jesus. Joseph's blood did not flow through Jesus' veins. It is a weird concept to think about. Joseph was chosen to raise a kid who was not biologically his own. And this kid had the greatest calling of any human being in existence.

We are called to raise our own kids, and many times we feel disqualified. But we are also called to father a generation that does not have our blood flowing through its veins. As Joseph did, if you say yes, a generational blessing will come. Jesus inherited Joseph's genealogy.

This is what God wants to give through you as a father to the next generation. For every kid who grew up without a father, God is going to graft him or her into the family. And for those who have no spiritual lineage, your simple yes will give them one.

To Mothers

You are not just a stay-at-home mom. You are a trainer for the next generation. You may feel as if you have nothing to give, whether you are up all night changing diapers, feeding your children three meals a day, taking them to school and sports practice or trying to survive their teenage years.

You are the true heroes of our time. And you, too, are needed. Your voice matters. Will you take up your phone and let the love that only a mother can feel and give go beyond the four walls of your house into the hearts of a generation?

Mary, the mother of Jesus, was a teenager who was given a task that she did not choose. Her task had moments of fear, ridicule, shame and doubt. I mean, who would have believed her conception story? But her simple yes to God birthed the One who would defeat death, hell and the grave.

As a mother, it is time that you roar for the children of this nation. For too long, the devil has deceived the children in your family as well as the generation that resides on the other side of your door. Every day as you drop your kids off at school, you see the work of the enemy. I believe that God's divine plan for this generation is enlisting and reenlisting moms and dads. It is not relying on missionaries who are called into the occupation of ministry. It is the last stand in this generation. And God's secret weapon is the family.

Write History with Your Life

Maybe you are not a mom or a dad—but you are just as qualified. This book has made it into your hands for a reason. There is a reason why you might have teared up during certain chapters or why your heart was moved when reading stories. This is your invitation. This is your permission to be a part of the Great Commission. Let it be said that we wrote history with our lives and that our lives counted for something. May your life count for something. I invite you to be a digital missionary. Preach the Gospel to the ends of the earth!

YOUR DIGITAL MISSION

Take all the wisdom you can get. Allow God to form you through His Word and through the leaders He has placed in your life. Stand boldly, live humbly, live holy, live simply. Give a yes to God every single day.

Remember to access the training resources at brianbar celona.com/dontscroll/.

Acknowledgments

Marcela, my wife, thank you for your encouragement and your love. Thank you for pushing me to lead even in moments that I did not want to. You truly are my best friend.

My children, thank you for your love and support. I loved how you would wait for me outside my office door asking, "Are you done yet?"

Pastor Netz Gomez, thank you for fathering me and for believing in me all these years.

Kala Maclain Boss, thank you for the countless hours you spent helping me write and edit this book. You are truly a blessing to my wife, to me and to my family.

Michael and Lorisa Miller, thank you for opening your lives up to our family and for UpperRoom being the incredible church of which we have been able to be a part.

Cynthia, thanks for being a mother to my wife and me, for your years of support and encouragement and for always hearing God at the right times.

How to Lead Someone to Christ

How to Share the Gospel

The Gospel is powerful! Romans 1:16 says that it is the power of God at work to save everyone who believes. In chapter 5, I encouraged you to preach a Gospel that calls people to give their lives wholeheartedly to Christ with one hundred percent allegiance to Him and obedience to His Word. As you think about the content you want to share, I recommend utilizing a combination of these two approaches:

1. **Social discipleship toward conversion.** Share your story and the truths about God's attributes, His Word and the principles of His Kingdom before you introduce people to Christ. This process plants seeds and moves people toward following Christ before they have given their hearts to Him.

2. **Straightforward invitation to follow Jesus.**

   a. Share your story/testimony of what God did and how He changed your life.

   b. Explain that there is a Kingdom that will continue for eternity and that Jesus is the door into that reality.

   c. Help people pray to receive Christ as Savior and Lord. Remember that accepting Christ is not just praying a prayer asking Jesus to come live in their heart. It is asking Jesus to lead their life, and then submitting to follow Him and obey His commands.

I also recommend that you include the following elements. Although you may not include all of these in every video, these four elements should represent your videos when seen together as one message.

- **Brokenness.** Be specific, vulnerable and relatable. Anyone can relate to brokenness, and people will find themselves somewhere in your story. Humanity is broken and requires a Savior and a leader. People can argue Bible principles with you, but people cannot argue about your story. Your openness about your humanity allows the divinity of God to shine on another's brokenness.

- **The nature of God.** Share the part of God's character that met you in your weakness. If you are struggling with anxiety, for example, share how Jesus is the Prince of Peace. Contrast your brokenness to the character of God. Then say, "Jesus died on a cross and rose from the dead to heal your brokenness and free you from sin."

- **An invitation**: Ask the question, "Will you give your life to Jesus, the One who is here to heal and help you?"

- **A response**: Explain that giving their life to Jesus means turning from their own self-focused way of doing things. Invite them to give exclusive and whole-hearted allegiance to God, to be passionate in their pursuit of Him and to be obedient to His Word.

Notes

Introduction

1. Roberts Liardon, *Frank Bartleman's Azusa Street* (Shippensburg, PA: Destiny Image Publishers, 2006).
2. "This Date in History—the 75th Anniversary of Television," *BillyGrahamLibrary.org*, April 30, 2014, https://billygrahamlibrary.org/this-date-in-history-the-75th-anniversary-of-television/.

Chapter 2: Live with No Plan B

1. You can read my full story in my book *The Jesus Club*. Brian Barcelona, *The Jesus Club* (Minneapolis: Chosen, 2017).

Chapter 4: Digital Missions

1. An Instagram live is a livestream broadcast or interview during which a few individuals discuss various topics on Instagram.

Chapter 5: What Is the Gospel?

1. Strong's Concordance, "2588. Karia," *BibleHub.com*, 2021, https://biblehub.com/greek/2588.htm.
2. To learn more about Progressive Christianity, read the linked article from *Christianity Today*. Jessica Knell, "Countering Progressive Christianity," *ChristianityToday.com*, July 29, 2020, https://www.christiantoday.com/article/countering.progressive.christianity/135286.htm.

Chapter 6: Long-Term Evangelism

1. This documentary can be viewed at https://sheepamongwolvesfilm
.com.

Chapter 10: Decentralized and Unified

1. "Decentralize," *Lexico.com*, 2021, https://www.lexico.com/en/defi
nition/decentralize.

Brian Barcelona is the founder of One Voice Student Missions and author of *The Jesus Club*. A leader on the forefront of youth evangelism, Brian is calling the high school students of America to surrender their lives to Jesus, and he is calling the Church to our nation's most unreached mission field: public high schools. Brian lives with his wife, Marcela, and their three children in Dallas, Texas. Connect with Brian at https://linktr.ee/brianbarcelona.

More from Brian Barcelona

When a teenage convert from atheism hears God calling him to action, he accepts the challenge despite his trepidation—and becomes the catalyst God uses to bring ongoing revival to high schools in America. This amazing true-life story will inspire you to believe that God can do wonderful things through you, if you simply obey!

The Jesus Club

 **Chosen**

 Stay up to date on your favorite books and authors with our free e-newsletters. Sign up today at chosenbooks.com.

 facebook.com/chosenbooks

 @Chosen_Books

 @chosen_books